MAKING DISCIPLES OF JESUS CHRIST

Implementing Effective Discipleship Strategies for Today's Church

Dr. Victor Oludiran

MAKING DISCIPLES OF JESUS CHRIST

Implementing Effective Discipleship Strategies for Today's Church

Copyright @ 2014 by Victor Oludiran

Unless otherwise specified, all Scripture quotations in this book are from The Holy Bible, King James Version. KJV is public domain in the United States printed in 1987.

Quoted Scriptures not indicated in the text are referenced in "Scripture References" (p145-149).

Victor Oludiran
LICAIM PUBLISHING
1851 Airport Industrial Park Dr.
Marietta GA, 30350, USA
admin@licaim.org
www.licaim.org

Printed in the United States of America

MAKING DISCIPLES
OF JESUS CHRIST

DEDICATION

To the loving memory of my late father, Rev J. L. A. Ogundiran, the first servant of God I grew up to know as a dedicated promoter of God's kingdom on earth, and a committed and passionate teacher of Christ's disciples.

To my Lord and Savior Jesus Christ who extended His saving grace to someone like me. I keep wondering what would have been my lot if I had not known Him.

ACKNOWLEDGMENTS

This work did not just evolve. It is a systematic product of many years of research that culminated in my doctorate degree in Ministry at Liberty University, Lynchburg, USA. I am grateful to all who supported and assisted me every step of the way, including my colleagues, friends, and instructors, especially Dr. Charlie Davidson and Dr. David Hirschman who were directly involved in the research project as my mentors.

The development and production of this book actually started with the suggestion of my friend, Dr. Dejo Afolayan, who had been involved in this research right from its formative stage and felt that I should develop the research findings into a book. He believed, as well as I do, that the materials contained in this project would help church leaders to develop their churches, as they focus on developing their members into leadership positions rather than counting them as ordinary members on the pew on Sundays. For Dejo's suggestion and contributions, I am profoundly grateful.

I also feel a deep sense of gratitude to the following people who were involved one way or the other in the research program, and in the production of this book. First and foremost is my lovely wife, best friend and my number one cheerleader over the years, Abimbola. I thank you for believing in my ability to succeed despite the various challenges at home and in the ministry. I also thank my children, Wale, Ronke, Yemi, and Doyin, and their spouses who encouraged and supported me throughout the program, and were involved in the formatting and editing processes of the manuscript.

I cannot forget the wise counsel of my friend, Pastor Michael Adebiyi of Jubilee Christian Church, Atlanta Georgia, who encouraged me in 2008 to be a person of value by seeking knowledge. Your wise counsel has obviously yielded some good fruits after some years of hard work, for which I am profoundly grateful.

It is practically impossible to mention all those who have contributed to both the research project and this book, due to space constraint. However, I want to identify the following people: Dr. Femi Adekunle, Rev (Dr.) Abel Ige, Mr. Atanda, Sunday Adegbola, and Dr. Adejoke Adenekan. I thank you all from my heart for your love, encouraging words, and prayers. I also want to appreciate the contribution of Dr. Mark Hardgrove, my departmental chair at Beulah Heights University,

Atlanta Georgia, where I am an adjunct faculty, who took the time to review the manuscript, and wrote the foreword to the book.

I want to recognize the love and support of my church family at Liberty Care International Ministries, the platform that God has provided for me to test and implement the structures and systems suggested in this book. You have demonstrated that these propositions are not mere intellectual adventure, but are of practical application. By your support and trust in the vision that God has given me, you have shown that there is no one God cannot use for His work, and there is no ministry God has established that He cannot make fruitful, with the right people and the right environment for growth. Thank you for your unflinching support.

TABLE OF CONTENTS

LIST OF TABLES

Foreword

As Dr. Oludiran notes at the beginning, the role of the church is not merely to make converts but to make disciples who then become effective reproductive members of the Body of Christ. Too often it seems that churches are content to fill the pews without considering whether the people in the pews are going beyond the walls of the church to reach the harvest. Dr. Oludiran has conducted research that explores the methodology of various churches for retaining and training visitors to become leaders. His insights are important with respect to the diverse approaches used by churches in his study, and his conclusions are helpful for any pastor that seeks to be more effective in the transformational process of leading a first time guest, to convert, to disciple and finally to leader.

Dr. Oludiran's organic approach to the church reveals that a holistic approach that integrates members into a meaningful organic whole can become a dynamic force for growth and kingdom effectiveness. Likewise, his summary of essential leadership qualities needed to lead such a church is helpful and instructive. Finally, Dr. Oludiran's insights relative to developing fruitful churches, is practical and certainly relevant for churches that are struggling to find a formula for effective growth that can become self-sustaining.

This work is for pastors that desire to do more than fill pews. It is a book that challenges church leaders to think holistically and to articulate a vision that is in alignment with the Great Commission. Dr. Oludiran dares churches and leaders to put a plan together that will honor God and will impact the kingdom by raising up leaders and insuring the future success of the church.

I encourage pastors to give this book a read and to honestly assess their own efforts relative to the mission that Christ gave the church. This book calls the church to return to the biblical mandate of the church to make disciples of all nations and to grow organically as members of the Body of Christ. If there has ever been a time when the church needs to return to these fundamentals, it is now.

Mark E. Hardgrove, PhD, D.Min
Senior Pastor of Conyers Church of God
& Chair of the Department of Business and
Leadership at Beulah Heights University

Introduction

In every aspect of life, leadership occupies a conspicuous position. An organization cannot exist without a leader. However, people conceive the concept of leadership in different ways. If a typical church leader is asked how his or her church is fairing, his/her response would probably be based on some quantitative assessment. For example, a church leader asked such a question is very likely to make known the number of worshippers that attended the worship service on Sundays. He/she also would likely want to determine the church's buoyancy by the dollar amount on the church's budget that was passed for the year, the large chunk of which is likely to be used for salaries, remunerations, and church maintenance.

Another aspect of the church that the pastor would mention is how effective their programs had been in attracting people most of whom are likely to be worshippers from other neighboring churches. When these and similar criteria of the pastor's assessment are considered to be above average, he or she would probably rate the church's overall performance as very impressive.

From this typical example of a pastor's assessment of a church's performance, it could be seen clearly that today's church has missed out completely on understanding its basic criteria for assessing its functionality and assignment. The church's primary assignment, which is commonly referred to as the Great

Commission, is also the church's marching order, specifying its responsibility to "go and make disciples of nations, teaching them to observe all that I have commanded you" (Matt 28:19). It is important to note that this divine statement has four elements in it:

First, "Go,"

Second, "Make Disciples,"

Third, "Baptize," and

Fourth, "Teach."

Some theologians believe that of the four elements, only one is imperative (a verb of command), while the other three are participles. The command is "make disciples." This is the sole responsibility of the church, and everything the church does and the assessment of its performance should be determined on the basis of this overarching goal. Although, quantitative assessment of the church could be useful for some other purposes, the best assessment of determining the growth, vibrancy, and impact of the church should be based on how effective the church is in making disciples.

There is no doubt that some churches give some attention to disciple making through some purposely designed training programs. However, the quality of the disciples they make is another issue entirely. It is doubtful if such disciples could stand the test of *true* disciples as scripturally prescribed. The church's loss of focus of its primary responsibility, and its shoddy attitude in raising true disciples has culminated in the loss of its vibrancy and relevance in the society. Take the American churches for example, it is estimated that 80 to 85 percent of the churches in America are in decline, and therefore need some degree of spiritual renewal.[1]

Clearly, churches are failing because they are not teaching people to observe all that Jesus has commanded. Until they redirect their efforts to the main assignment of raising disciples, there is no amount of attractive programs or other efforts that could make them get out of their state of decline and irrelevance. The purpose of this book therefore, is to assert the fact that the church's pitiable condition is attributed to its neglect of the Great Commission of making disciples, which has made the church fall short of expectation. In order to restore the church back on its divine course of operation, this book will proffer a system whereby churches could grow systematically and exponentially by moving their congregation from nominal membership to spiritual maturity.

Why this Book?

This book is designed to describe the effectiveness of the church in making disciples as they aspire to fulfill the Great Commission. It is clear that many church leaders have completely lost focus of their assignment to make disciples; and the program of discipleship which those who make the attempt to do have in place is inadequate, unimplemented, or both. The consequence is the declining or dying state of the churches.

Studies confirm that "Some churches have plateaued, and in decline while others are in the last stages of dying."[2] Aubrey Malphurs describes the state of health of a typical church as desperate, and therefore, needs urgent attention. He metaphorically presents the spiritual state of the church when he writes, "If the typical church were to go to a hospital emergency the attending physician would likely admit it to the hospital and put it on life support." He argued that the vast majority of churches in America had plateaued, or in a state of utter decline. He further predicted that of the 400,000 churches in the country, as many as 350,000 could close their doors."[3]

It is generally believed that America, like some Western countries is fast becoming a post-Christian nation with declining interest in biblical Christian matters. This could be blamed on the church, not the people because it has been observed that "the people are interested in spiritual matters, only they regard today's churches as out of touch and therefore, have no answer to their spiritual, physical and emotional needs."[4] The overall picture of the church today does not seem to point to its ability to fulfill its God-given duty of making disciples of all nations.

For the church to be restored back to health and be made relevant in the society, it should be in a position of producing zealots for Christ who would be able to transform the world. In the words of George Barna, Zealots are "individuals who are intractably devoted to knowing, loving, and serving God with all their heart, mind, strength, and soul."[5] Therefore, fulfilling the Great Commission goes beyond winning some souls for Christ; it involves developing those souls to spiritual maturity, and making them stand out as disciple producers of godly character and are poised to transform their world for Christ.

Some theologians believe that the church as a living organism has a life span of forty years from its birth through maturity, to its eventual decline and ultimate death. This is much likely to happen when a church has no system of progressive discipleship and succession. However, when the church adopts a system of continuity in developing disciples and leaders, it becomes a cycle of constant growth and progress, without a point of decline or termination. Paul's advice to Timothy makes this point relevant and clearer, "And the things that thou hast heard of among many witnesses, the same commit thou to faithful men, who shall be able to teach others also" (2 Tim 2:2). In this text, Paul is advising Timothy to create a cycle of disciples, which is to guarantee at least three levels of leadership successions.

What This Book is Not

It is important to place a disclaimer on the relevance of this book to today's church. First of all, it is descriptive, not prescriptive. This is because in it I look at some problems of the church from a relatively broad vantage point. Therefore, it is not talking about one particular church, unlike when Paul wrote to and spoke specifically about churches in Rome, Corinth, Galatians, Ephesus, Philippi, Colossae, and Thessalonica, or when John wrote concerning the seven churches in Asia Minor in the Book of Revelation. This book and the ideas espoused in it may not necessarily be applicable to any particular church situation.

Second, this book does not intend to present a formulaic model of church growth through discipling people, but it is to offer ideas for growth and because of its foundation in biblical principles, these ideas could be applicable to some churches, irrespective of location or culture. In other words, this book does not produce a one-size-fits-all model.

Third, this book is not necessarily about church administration and leadership. It is written with the idea that there is a bilateral relationship between the spiritual and the sociological, which could be utilized by God's servants to facilitate growth. Yet, it does not prescribe or explain the methods and quality of leadership that would enable the church to accomplish this goal.

Fourth, this book does not pretend to predict the behavior of people in their responses to the gospel message. Predicting a common pattern of behavior for all people in all kinds of culture and environment could be misleading. Lastly, this book recognizes the supernatural intervention of the Holy Spirit, which may bring about the growth of a church or spur its decline regardless of humanly explicable circumstances.

An Overview

This book is divided into seven chapters. *Chapter one* establishes the basis of the book. Following the introduction, it highlights basic topics like biblical and pastoral theologies, understanding critical concepts, statement of methodology, and what the Bible and other people have been saying on the subject of discipleship.

Chapter two focuses on the concept of disciple and discipleship, offering suitable definitions for both terms so as to help church leaders to have a clear understanding of these terms. With a clear understanding, the leaders would be able to identify a disciple whenever they see one, and would also be able to set up a suitable methodology for producing them. *Chapter three* does the same thing for the concept of leaders and leadership.

Since a new convert is not usually ready-made for church responsibilities, but must have to go through the process of growth, *Chapter four* establishes the structure of growth through which a disciple could be best developed. As a book having its basis in research methodology, *Chapter five* reveals the research findings conducted on some sampled American churches based on some factors like, the church's vision, training and development programs, evangelism programs, and their small group structures. I suggest you skip this chapter if you are not research inclined.

Chapter six discusses the health of the church as a body, based on the health of the individual parts that make it up. What makes up the health of the parts is also considered as the kind of food the pastor feeds the congregation with, which ultimately determines the kind of body the church would have.

Chapter seven looks at the analogy of the Vine and its branches, and considers how believers could produce much fruit as they abide in the Vine, and the role of the church to make them accomplish this.

Chapter eight concludes with God's reward system, and how everyone would expect to give account of the good works he/she puts up while here on earth. Taking a cue from the Parable of the Talent, our fruitfulness and profitability is what gives God glory.

CHAPTER 1

Biblical and Pastoral Theologies

This book is rooted in both biblical and pastoral theologies. These two perspectives are explained in the next few paragraphs.

Biblical Theology

This book has its basis in the Scriptures, emphasizing believers' task in converting unbelievers, and making them disciples who are able to produce other disciples. The biblical references are traceable to the Great Commandment, the Great Commission, and the New Commandment. These three fundamentals constitute the disciple's mode of operation. Understanding these passages would make church leaders appreciate the foundational requirements for discipleship.

The Great Commandment

This is the Great Commandment as recorded in the Book of Matthew,

> *But when the Pharisees had heard that he had put the Sadducees to silence, they were gathered together. Then one of them, which was a lawyer,*

asked him a question, tempting him, and saying,
Master, which is the great commandment in the
law? Jesus said unto him, Thou shalt love the
Lord thy God with all thy heart, and with all thy
soul, and with all thy mind. This is the first and
great commandment. And the second is like unto
it, Thou shalt love thy neighbor as thyself. On
these two commandments hang all the law and
the prophets (Matt 22:34-40).

The first commandment is to love God totally, with all one's being. The second commandment is for believers to love their neighbors as themselves. Jesus sums up all the laws of the Old Testament into these two. It is therefore, important for anyone who wants to be a disciple of Jesus to know how to express love to God, and to others because these are the reflections of God's nature, for God is love.

The Great Commission

This is the prime mission of not just the church, but also every Christian. It is found with varying emphasis in the four gospels, and the Book of Acts. Matthew states,

Go ye therefore, and teach all nations, baptizing
them in the name of the Father, and of the Son,
and of the Holy Ghost; teaching them to observe
all things whatsoever I have commanded you;

and lo, I am with you always, even unto the end of the world (Matt 28:19-20).

This Scripture, which appears to be the most famous commission, has as the command, "make disciples," and is connected to three participles: go, baptize, and teach. The fulfillment of this task is supported by Jesus' promise that He will be with them until the end of the age. Matthew's emphasis in this text is disciple making, which entails the process of developing individuals and helping them to observe the commands of Jesus. Until churches are involved in this task passionately, they may never be able to make disciples as they should, which is the bane of today's church. This is why the command to make disciples must be understood to mean that we must help people not only to confess Jesus Christ as their Lord and Savior, but help them develop a life of true discipleship.

In Mark we read,

And he said unto them, Go ye unto all the world and preach the gospel to every creature. He that believeth and is baptized shall be saved; but he that believeth not shall be damned (Mk 16:15-16).

This passage outlines the scope of the mission, *all the world* and *every creation.*

In Luke's account we read:

And he said unto them, These are the words which I spake unto you, while I was yet with you, that all things must be fulfilled, which were

*written in the law of Moses, and in the prophets
and in the psalms, concerning me. And said unto
them, thus it is written, and thus it behoves
Christ to suffer and to rise from the dead the
third day; and that repentance and remission of
sins should be preached in his name among   all
nations, beginning at Jerusalem. And ye are
witnesses of these things (Lk 24:44-49).*

The task of the disciples in this text is to be witnesses of Jesus as they proclaim the message of repentance for the forgiveness of sins, which is the theme of this passage. "You are witnesses of these things" (v. 49), entails the disciples bearing witness of Christ's death and resurrection.

The Gospel of John states, "Then said Jesus to them again, Peace be unto you: as my Father hath sent me, even so send I you" (Jn 20:21). This text emphasized the theoretical nature of the sending, which is to make believers see Jesus' mission as their mission, and delivering the message in an atmosphere of peace.

The same author of the gospel of Luke states as recorded in the Book of Acts,

*But ye shall receive power, after that the Holy
Spirit is come upon you: and ye shall be witnesses
unto me, both in Jerusalem, and in all Judea, and
in Samaria, and unto the uttermost part of the
earth (Acts 1:8).*

It is not surprising that this text, authored by Luke, has the same context of witnessing and proclamation of the good news.

The promise of the Holy Spirit was fulfilled at Pentecost following which the efforts of the disciples to carry out the commission are expressed throughout the book as confirmation. This shows that the believers' task of making disciples cannot be done in their own power and efforts. They need the empowerment of the Holy Spirit so that they could perform extraordinarily beyond the limits of their own power. In summary, the Great Commission is an essential part of the gospel. Without it, the gospel is incomplete.[16]

The New Commandment

Jesus spoke exclusively to His disciples as he gave them the New Commandment,

> *"A new commandment I give unto you, that ye love one another; as I have loved you, that ye also love one another. By this shall all men know that ye are my disciples, if ye have love one to another" (Jn 13:34-35).*

Here, Jesus gave the disciples what looks like their identification mark: loving one another. It is with this identification that other people would recognize them as disciples of Christ. This is perhaps what the people of Antioch observed when the disciples were referred to as

Christians for the first time. The meaning of *Christian* is *follower of Christ*, (*Christianos*), Strong's G5546).

The implication is that when Christians love one another, it would serve as an invitation to other people, and make the people, including unbelievers gravitate towards them. Paul states the same concept thus, "Let love be without dissimulation. Abhor that which is evil; cleave to that which is good. Be kindly affectioned one to another with brotherly love; in honor preferring one another" (Rom 12:9-10). Therefore, the Christian's first step in demonstrating the love of Christ is to let it reflect in the way they love other Christians and others outside the fold.

In a nutshell, Christians are to love God, love their neighbors, and love other brothers and sisters in Christ, and unbelievers. Love is the central component in the kingdom of God. God loved the world so much that He sent His Son to come and die for our sins. Therefore, Christians must first love God because when they love God whom they do not see, it would be easy for them to love their neighbors, and other believers whom they see.

Pastoral Theology

The thrust of this book has an aspect of pastoral theology in it, which must be clearly stated for emphasis. To start with, let us look at Jesus' statement to His disciples, "Follow me, and I will make you fishers of men" (Matt 4:19). The disciples who were *ordinary* men followed Jesus for three years, and turned their world upside down as they went about carrying out the Great Commission.

In the same way, church leaders are expected to transform their followers such that they too would be able to transform their world, which the process of discipleship is all about. However, we know that only a handful of evangelical church members are involved in making disciples of those who are led to Christ. This sad fact portrays our modern day church as delinquent in their basic responsibility of transforming converts and members to disciples of Christ. Until church leaders take discipleship as a passionate and urgent command that it is, they are not going to be able to experience the kind of growth and multiplication that God expects from them. This involves a systematic and formal process. The hope is that this book will help church leaders to think more deeply about this serious process that the Lord Himself has designed for all His children to follow so that they could truly make disciples of all nations.

Critical Concepts

Central to the work of discipleship are concepts that every church leader must have as the rule of thumb. Some of them are familiar while others are not. In what follows, I will explain some of them.

Small Groups

Small groups are individual units within the church that function for the overall building of the larger body. Jeffrey Arnold defines small group as, "An intentional gathering of a varied number of people who commit themselves to regular meetings for the purpose of becoming better disciples of Jesus Christ."[1] Jeffrey identified the basic purpose of small groups as "the need to build community."[2] He attributes the accomplishment of the early church to their operation as house churches. The basic principles that are peculiar with small groups are that they are intentional, relational, and they involve regular meetings. Their goal is to make disciples of Christ, elevate the efforts of the larger church, and alleviate the burden of anonymity which members of a growing church may experience in their journey to true maturity.

Home Cell Groups

This term, which is made popular by Paul Yonggi Cho, the pastor of the world's largest congregation in Seoul, South Korea, is used in this book synonymously with small groups because they represent the same kind f gathering of people, who are gathered for the same purpose of developing disciples and leaders, and growing the Body of Christ. According to Cho, "In the cell groups, each one has an opportunity to be used by God to minister to the others in the group."[3] This is what sets the home cell group apart from church congregation coming together on Sundays.

Disciple

Grammatically, the word *disciple* is both an action verb and a noun. In its noun form, it means a learner, follower, adherent, and supporter. In the verb form, the same word could mean anything in the range of, to bring up, to raise, to nurture to maturity, to mentor, to grow, to groom, to lead, and to train. The biblical example is Jesus' call to His disciples with the promise that He would make them *fishers of men.* This is why Jesus made it an inevitable commitment for His disciples to teach people to observe all things that He has commanded them. Therefore, the mark of discipleship goes beyond being a Christian or a church member. It requires sacrifice and commitment. Details of the requirements and commitments for discipleship will be discussed in Chapter two.

There is no doubt that discipleship is the basis of the believer's faith in Christ because they are not called into church membership, but are called as Christ's disciples. Oswald Sander observes, "It is not without significance that the word *disciple* occurs in the New Testament 269 times, *Christian* only three times, and *believer*, two times. This surely indicates that the task of the church is not so much to make 'Christians' or 'believers' but 'disciples.'"[4]

Discipleship

The process of transforming a convert to a true disciple is what discipleship is all about. Barna defines *discipleship* as "becoming a complete and competent follower of Jesus Christ."[5] This is precariously the missing ingredient in today's church, for leaders are more interested in making members than making disciples. As a result, the church has missed the divine order to *go and make disciples of nations*. Barna further observes, "Disciple making is not optional. The strength and influence of the church is wholly dependent upon its commitment to true discipleship. Producing transformed lives and seeing those lives reproduced in others, is a core challenge to believers, and to the local church."[6] It is that missing ingredient for transforming converts to true disciples that this book is set out to provide.

Leader

The biblical understanding of a leader is someone who is in God's service to serve without the motivation of persona gains. For instance, Jesus' teaching on leadership specifies, "Whoever wants to be a leader shall be the servant of all" (Mk 10:44). Therefore, anyone who does not have the heart of service is not fit to be a leader. This concept is contrary to the secular understanding of a leader as someone who is at the helm of affairs, dictating the shots. The biblical concept is what his book will emphasize, especially in the discussion and nature of a leader, in Chapter three.

Leadership

The process of making a leader is what leadership is all about. Since the church has different kinds of strategies for making leaders, it follows that there must also be different kinds of leaders that the church would produce. It is for the purpose of making biblical proven leaders that this book proffers a specific strategy that is considered effective in its effects in Chapter four.

Saints

In Paul's writings, he referred to his converts in the churches he founded in Corinth, Ephesus, and Philippians as *saints*. Thus, by this understanding, believers of every denomination and creed are regarded as saints. The Bible makes it clear that the ministry gifts of apostles, prophets, evangelists, pastors, and teachers are given to the church "for the perfecting of the saints" (Eph 4:12). *Saints* in this context refers to believers. This term does not categorize believers, but puts them all at the same level. This term will be used throughout this book in this context.

Gospel

The Greek word, *euangelion* means "the Gospel" or "the good news." But the question is, why is the gospel called good news? "Good news" in terms of what? Well, the good news being talked about here is the good news of God's plan for the salvation of mankind, which God perfected through the sacrifice of Jesus Christ on the Cross for the forgiveness of sin and the promise of eternal life. The Books of the Bible that give accounts of the birth, life, death, and resurrection of Jesus Christ are also referred to as the Gospel. These Books are: Matthew, Mark, Luke, and John. When the message of the New Testament is preached, it is sometimes referred to as preaching the Gospel, especially when Jesus is the subject or focus of the message.

Vision/dream

Functionally, these two concepts are different from each other but not mutually exclusive. As metaphors, a dream is a stream of subconscious or unconscious imagination, while a vision is a realizable imagination or feasible thoughts. In this book, the two terms are used interchangeably. Every life purpose starts from a vision; so also is every ministry that God has ordained, because it is vision that gives impetus to purpose. This book will adopt the definition of vision by George Barna. He defines vision as "a clear special image of a probable future implanted by God to His chosen servants, and is based upon an accurate understanding of God, self, and circumstances."[7]

The Bible says, "Where there is no vision, the people perish" (Prov 29:18). It is because of the importance of vision in leadership that I will explore the extent to which church leaders are motivated by their vision in Chapter five, and how such vision has contributed to the growth of their church or otherwise.

Church

The concept of church as reflected in this book is not the common notion of church as a building. When someone says that he/she is going to church, the understanding is that the person is going into a building or a place of worship. However, the original meaning of *church* (*ekklesia*) used in Pauline epistles as *people of God in congregation* would be adopted in this book. The word ekklesia literally refers to church as the *called out ones.* This means the church is 'called out' from the world by God and "called out" to proclaim His greatness.

Statement of Methodology

This book advocates the preparation and development of members for service as true disciples, including soul winning. As earlier pointed out, making disciples, which is a major goal of the Great Commission, is often neglected by the church. Thus, as would be seen later in the research findings, today's church is not all that effective in its program of discipling nations. another research finding noted, that "just one percent of adult believers contend that they have the spiritual gift of evangelism; while less than one-tenth (of the adult believers) said they have never intentionally built a relationship with someone in the hope of being able to lead the person to Christ."[8] This is not an encouraging report, but an indictment on the abysmal failure of the Body of Christ in developing members to matured disciples for soul winning.

On the side of the unchurched, the same report noted, "Most unchurched people have never been invited to a church by a Christian," and that "most unchurched people have never been told by a Christian what it means to believe in Jesus Christ and never invited to embrace Jesus as their Lord and Savior."[9] It is little wonder why revivals tarry in the church around the world today.

Another noticeable reflection of the church's inability to positively influence the spiritual growth of their members is in their lifestyles, commitments, and habits. Studies have also shown that the church is not doing much in this area because, only "a small number reported that their church helps them develop specific paths to follow to foster spiritual growth."[10] The same report finds that "only 20 percent of members believe that their church has some means of facilitating an evaluation of the spiritual/commitment to maturing of the congregation."[11]

On the positive side, two noticeable features distinguish churches that make concrete efforts in developing their members and disciples to maturity. First, they are structurally organized for the purpose of effectively transforming and developing members' skills and abilities that reflect Christian lifestyle and responsibilities. An example is the North Point

Community Church in Alpharetta, Georgia, which through stimulation of small groups grew from a house fellowship to 12,000 congregants. The pastor, Andy Stanley, in attesting to the members' small group involvement says,

> What we discover is that sustained spiritual growth is not well nurtured by an environment where people simply sit in rows, listening to messages in complete anonymity. Sustained growth takes place where people are personally challenged and encouraged in their relationship with God, and others. This is especially true when the challenges of life occur, and eventually challenges come to everyone.[12]

Second, the churches have structured developmental programs for training and mentoring members. In such programs, the church is able to identify and develop their members' potentials and gifting for effective Christian life and responsibilities.

In helping the church leaders to revitalize their churches, the descriptive method has been used in this research work to ascertain the effectiveness or otherwise of some churches' methods of making disciples. The purpose is to determine the effectiveness or otherwise of this method. This is based on the proposition that "a church that engages in effective discipleship is a church that will grow steadily and solidly. This is because people love to be cared for; and a church that emphasized genuine spiritual care and facilitates real spiritual growth will be a magnet."[26]

In preparation for this book, I designed a survey to identify the discipleship models of 20 churches as well as the effectiveness of such models. This is to help develop a benchmark aimed at assisting churches' leaders move their congregations from nominal membership to true disciples. In this process, some hypothesis emerged:

1. The more the convert becomes a converter, the more likely the church will grow.

2. The more dynamic the church's training and development curriculum is, the more likely levels of disciples will emerge.

3. The level of active engagement of a church in discipleship efforts will determine the extent of its growth or a lack thereof.

4. The vision of a church leadership is directly proportional to the rate of its success in soul winning and membership growth.

5. Churches with small group ministry will develop spiritually mature members who are able to identify and express their gifts and calling, reflecting in the overall health and vibrancy of the church.

I hope that as pastors and leaders think of these ideas, and apply the principles highlighted in this book, they would be able to move their churches from where they are to where God wants them to be.

What Others Have Been Saying

A church practice as old and fundamental as discipleship would certainly have much literature credited to it. Some of such volumes explain specific church models which the church leaders claimed had given their churches the expected surge in growth and vibrancy. An example is Andy Stanley, the pastor of the North Point Community Church, Alpharetta in Atlanta, who described how he built a church of 12,000 attendees through the small group model, in which members are encouraged to spend time together. As members operate in small groups, Stanley believes that they experience spiritual growth as evident in their relationship with God and man.

Another volume in which the authors detailed their small group experience in building their church is in the 1997 work of Glen Martin and Gary McIntosh titled, *Creating Community: Deeper Fellowship through Small Group Ministry*. In this seminal work, the authors deposed that every Christian needs another person for a victorious Christian journey, and strongly advocate small group relationship among Christians as a way of life.

Earley and Rod Dempsey also wrote an excellent volume entitled, *The Pocket Guide to Leading a Small Group, (*Houston: *TX,* Touch Publications, 2007*)*. This *Pocket Guide* includes 52 ways to help leaders grow their small group. This is a practical book as the proposed principles had been tried and tested successfully by the authors in their church, New Life Church in Gahanna, Ohio. This is a must-read for every church leader who aspires to build his/her church on small group structure.

An outstanding resource is *Successful Home Cell Groups* by Yonggi Cho, (Gainesville, FL: Bridge-Logos Publishers, 1981), which is a practical approach to home cell group structure by a man who used the system to grow what is now known as the largest church in the world. Cho believes that the system which worked for him in his church at Yoido Full Gospel Church in Seoul, South Korea could work for anyone anywhere in the world. This source explains the organizational structure and the visionary role of the Senior Pastor as the primary champion of the small group model, without which the system could not succeed.

A wonderful resource is *The Nine Keys to Effective Small Group Leadership,* by Carl George (Mansfield, PA: Kingdom publishing, 1997). The sections on coaching and developing an apprentice are very helpful. In this book, George emphasizes the unlimited leadership potential of the members of the church which should be tapped for the fulfillment of the Great Commission.

Another outstanding book, *Turning Members into Leaders*, by Dave Earley, (Houston TX: Touch Publications, 2004), is a step-by-step strategy of doing exactly what the title suggests, turning members of the church into leaders instead of spectators. This book is designed to guide and help church leaders form small groups that give each member an opportunity to get involved in church ministry. The author emphasizes the developmental process, which every member of the church should go through in the process of developing their potentials.

In an inspiring interview in the *Leadership Journal 4* (*Fall 1988*) titled, "Can Spiritual Maturity be taught?" Roberta Hestenes, the President of Eastern College, agrees that pastors who are themselves trained to be in a position of training their members could particularly teach spiritual maturity. She saw the pastor as the spiritual director for the congregation and the person with the sole responsibility of nourishing the congregation into growth and spirituality. On the issue of church growth, Hestenes considered small groups as a favorable structure for growth. Hestenes' opinion on small groups goes a long way in shaping my thoughts in considering small groups as the pragmatic model for church growth and development of members.

In his work, *Tomorrow's Church: A Community of Change* (Waco, TX: World Books Publishers, 2001), John Westerhoff addresses the issue of Christian life from the point of view of the Creator. He made the unequivocal point that being a Christian is living as an agent of God in transforming the world into what God intends it to be. He interprets Jesus' call to His church as a call to be a community of change. Westerhoff believes that true conversion can only be accomplished when the groups and societies from where new converts come are transformed as well, otherwise the new converts would revert to their old ways.

In his book, *Missional Reformation for Discipling Nations,* (Houston TX: Omega Publishers, 2009), Abi Olowe, writing from the empirical knowledge of God Embassy Church in Kiev Ukraine, highlights the organization of the church in small groups and the systematic training of members for discipleship and ministry. Olowe detailed the spiritual progress of some members of the church, many of whom were discovered by the church when they were addicts, alcoholics, prostitutes, and generally with hopeless situations. However, these people were saved, discipled, and became productive members, church planters and influencers of their communities. This is a practical demonstration of the task of the church.

Aubrey Malphurs, writing from the perspective of a church consultant, in his volume titled, *A New Kind of Church: Understanding Models of Ministry for the 21st Century,* (Grand Rapids, MI: Baker Nooks, 2007), identifies the general state of the church as declining and therefore offers that the church needed to adopt a model that would bring the required growth and spirituality. This is because a church that is based on the structure that produces leaders would grow both numerically and spiritually.

One of the most helpful academic works done on this subject is Dempsey's Doctor of Ministry thesis, "A

Strategy to Transition a Traditional Church Educational System to a Small Group System" (2004). In it, Dempsey does a case study on the transformation that his church experienced as he and his pastor colleagues took the church from a traditional Sunday school model to a small group system, with outstanding growth. This work makes available the necessary principles that must be followed to experience the same result. The author also highlights some pitfall which must be avoided.

While many of these volumes touch on the theme of discipleship, leadership, and small group ministry, it is my aim to supplement these works with a descriptive study of a workable model of discipleship, which is the same as redirecting the attention of church leaders to the neglected or forgotten divine assignment of the church, which if adopted, is expected to move declining churches to health and vibrancy.

What the Bible Says

Some of the Scriptures that support the subject of discipleship and leadership shall be highlighted in this section to ascertain the fact that the subject is firmly rooted in the word of God, and that God has a way of guiding us into His basic truth. Take for instance God's call to Abraham, in which the Bible says,

Now the Lord had said unto Abram, Get thee out of thy country, and from thy kindred, and from thy father's house, unto a land that I will shew thee: And I will make of thee a great nation, and I will bless thee, and make thy name great; and thou shalt be a blessing: And I will bless them that bless thee, and curse him that curseth thee: and in thee shall all families of the earth be blessed (Gen 12: 1-3).

How is Abraham's call relevant to the subject of discipleship and leadership? It shows that God has a purpose of making something big out of something small and negligible, and by His power and direction, He makes His purpose come to realization. Just as God had a plan and purpose for Abraham who was called from an unimpressive background, so also does He have plan for everyone of us, irrespective of our background, culture or race. This is why the Christian journey should be taken seriously, always depending and relying on God's providence and direction, as people searching for their Promised Land.

The Great Commission, which our Lord Jesus gave to His disciples and by implication, to His church, highlights the centerpiece of this book. After Jesus had resurrected, and knew that all power had been given to Him in heaven and on the earth, He commissioned His disciples to make disciples of all nations of the world. The process that He laid out included baptizing and teaching the people all things He (Jesus Christ) had commanded them.

Jesus called His disciples "that they might be with Him" (Mk 3:14). For three years, Jesus established a deep and close relationship with the men such that they lived together, spent time together, ate meals together and travelled together. In other words, the disciples imbibed the Master's qualities and characteristics in their close interactions that other people easily identify them as people who had been with Jesus. This is the kind of effect which small group relationships is expected to have between the leader and members, and among members.

Paul has so much to say on the subject of discipleship and leadership. For example, he wrote to the Romans church,

> *Moreover whom he did predestinate, them he also called: and whom he called, them he also justified: and whom he justified, them he also glorified (Rom 8:28-30).*

This Scripture indicates God's plan which specifies that everyone is called, justified and glorified. This is why church leaders should take the issue of developing members seriously, rather than taking them as numbers making up their congregations. Thus, if God sees every Christian as called, justified and glorified, they should be treated as such.

Paul wrote the following words to the Philippians church,

> *And being found in fashion as a man, he humbled himself, and became obedient unto death, even the death of the cross. Wherefore God also hath highly exalted him, and given him a name which is above every name: That at the name of Jesus every knee should bow, of things in heaven, and things in earth, and things under the earth (Phil 2:8-10).*

Among the identified qualities of leadership humility is at the forefront without which one becomes unteachable. This is derived from Jesus' example as He "humbled himself, and became obedient unto death." Thus, every Christian should be humble, because the reward of humility is always enhanced in promotion.

Peter wrote in his epistle,

> *The elders which are among you I exhort, who am also an elder, and a witness of the suffering of Christ, and also a partaker of the glory that shall be revealed: Feed the flock of God which is among you, taking the oversight thereof, not by constraint, but willingly; not for filthy lucre, but of a ready mind (1 Pet 5:1-2).*

The basic responsibility of church leaders is spelt out

very clearly in this passage. The argument is simply that the health of the church will always be determined by the kind of spiritual food with which the pastor feeds the congregation. Thus, the work of ministry must be performed with clarity of purpose "to feed the flock of Christ" and not for personal gains.

Paul wrote to the church in Ephesus,

> *And he gave some, apostles; and some, prophets; and some, evangelists; and some, pastors; and some teachers; For the perfecting of the saints, for the work of the ministry, for the edifying of the body of Christ: Till we all come in the unity of the faith, and of the knowledge of the Son of God, unto a perfect man, unto the measure of the stature of the fullness of Christ (Eph 4: 11-13).*

This is another passage which clearly specifies the work of church leaders as *equipping* the saints. Paul likens the church to the *Body of Christ* and every church member to a particular part of the body, which has a specific function to perform. In other words, every church member must be seen as an important part that makes the body function effectively, and without which the body would be considered as incomplete or incapacitated. Thus, leaders must aspire to train everyone as people who have some contributions to make to the overall health of the body. Paul further asserts,

"From whom the whole body fitly joined together and compacted by that which e very joint supplieth, according to the effectual working in the measure of every part, maketh increase of the body unto the edifying of itself in love" (Eph 4:16).

The ultimate purpose of discipleship is figuratively described in the same context as a healthy body with all the parts in good working conditions. The weakness of one part affects the overall health of the whole. This is why the Bible emphasizes the task of the church leaders as keeping the Body healthy through proper nurturing of every member that collectively makes up the body. In another Paul's writing, he says,

And we proclaim Him, admonishing every man and teaching every man with all wisdom, that we may present every man complete in Christ (Col 1:28).

The subject of this text is *every man*, whom Paul says, must be presented complete in Christ. It is therefore, the church's responsibility to ensure spiritual growth for every believer, and not just a few people developed to lead church programs. As a result of the prominence and importance of these Scriptures, some of them will come up again in some sections of this book for emphasis.

CHAPTER 2

Discipleship

The Identity of a Disciple

It should not be assumed that every church leader operates with a clear understanding of who a disciple is. This explains why church leaders do not develop disciples of the same qualities. In other words, the divergent notions of the concept of discipleship have resulted in a diversity of disciples. For instance, a church leader could regard a new convert as a disciple, while another leader's notion of a disciple could be someone who sings in the choir, or teaches a Sunday school class, or even a volunteer in a church ministry. It would not be surprising if in some cases a church leader refers to a member of his congregation as his or her disciple.

What these divergent views suggest is that the church is yet to come up with a common understanding of the concept of a disciple. However, until the church understands, without any doubt who a disciple is, it is very likely that the church would be producing different kinds of products in the name of disciples. Incidentally, disciple making is the sole responsibility of the church, and if the church is not clear about who a disciple is, there would be problems in effectively carrying out her responsibilities.

This chapter will provide a common ground for the church's understanding of a disciple, and by implication, make the process of discipleship clearer with a working definition of the concepts of "disciple," and "discipleship" being formulated. This is important because if the seed of a tree is defective, the fruit it would produce would equally be defective, that is, if the plant that comes out of it germinates at all. Since this has been the missing link for the church, this book intends to provide an effective and applicable mould from which the perfect product of disciples could be made. I hope that from the working definition that this book will provide, the process of discipleship would be so clear that those who decide to follow the process would be sure of the kind of disciples that would come out of it.

Qualifications of a Disciple

As Jesus called His disciples, he had a picture of whom he wanted them to be in His mind, and that is why He invited them, "Follow me, and I will make you fishers of men" (Matt 4:19). Jesus wanted to "make" the disciples what he wanted them to be, so that they would have distinct features as Jesus' disciples. Thus, to "make" requires a process of transformation, which is expected to be accomplished as they follow Jesus not only physically, but also in His teachings and instructions. The disciples were to learn from the Master, as they imbibed His character, and values. The word *disciple* means "a learner" (Strong's H310). This means that the disciple is expected to take after the Master, called Rabbi in the culture of the time, as they watch and listen to Him, in their close interaction with Him.

Jesus, however, specifies some qualifications for anyone who was to be His disciple. It is not surprising that not everyone who wanted to follow Him qualified to be His disciple. It is also on record that Jesus called some people, who could not follow Him because they did not have the necessary qualifications. Therefore, the qualifications and requirements of a disciple were spelt out by Jesus Himself on different occasions in His ministry. Among others, Jesus specified the following qualifications:

A disciple must consider the cost

"For which of you, intending to build a tower, sitteth not down first, and counteth the cost, whether he have sufficient to finish it?" (Lk 14:28). To be a follower of Christ, one must count the cost because there is a price to pay. Gordon Ferguson describes the price as death.[1] He explains, "For the true disciple, it will cost you your life, your body, your possessions, and your future. It will cost you everything."[2] For him, death is an essential condition because apart from the fact that it could cost him his life, a disciple is expected to die to self, which means that he is not to seek self-satisfaction and personal gratification. Rather, he is to seek to please God daily and in everything he/she does. Therefore, being Jesus' disciple requires a deep and serious consideration because it would cost the person his own will and desires.

A disciple must be totally committed to Christ

"If any man come to me, and hate not his father, and mother, and wife, and children, and brethren, and sister, yea, and his own life also, he cannot be my disciple" (Lk 14:26). Jesus considers His relationship with His disciples to be so uncompromising that when compared with other relationships, it would appear like hatred. Jesus is using hyperbole, a figure of speech defined as deliberate exaggeration, to give effect to the seriousness of discipleship.

Therefore, hate should not be taken in the negative sense of it because Jesus is the embodiment of love, which he demonstrated by dying on the cross for our sins. What this statement means is that the love that a disciple would manifest to any other human would pale in comparison to the love he or she would show to the Lord Jesus Christ. Etymologically, the word, *discipline* and the word *disciple* come from the same root word. One cannot disciple someone who is undisciplined. Strictly following the Lord requires a great deal of discipline on the part of the disciple.

A disciple must surrender or die to self

"And whosoever doth not bear his cross and come after me cannot be my disciple" Lk 14:27). The symbol of the cross is representational of death and suffering. Therefore, to carry one's cross means that the disciple is willing to suffer or even lay down his/her life for his Master. What is emphasized here is serious commitment to the service of God. By being willing to give up his/her will and desires, the disciple is determined to follow Christ all the way whatever the Master demands, without looking back.

A disciple must give up all earthly possessions

"So likewise, whosoever he be of you that forsaketh not all that he hath, he cannot be my disciple" (Lk 14:33). A true disciple must consider all that he or she possesses to be held in trust for the Master; and whenever the Master calls for it, the disciple must surrender it. Whenever one finds it difficult to give up something for Christ, that thing has become that person's god. For this, Jesus said, "No man can serve two masters; for either he will hate the one and love the other, or else he will hold to the one, and despise the other. Ye cannot serve God and mammon" (Matt 6:24). Emptying oneself of his/her material possessions helps one to focus on God's service. Here, the Lord is emphasizing the need to break the yoke of the secular in exchange it for the holy. This is because, according to Him, "My yoke is easy, and my burden is light" (Matt 11:30).

A disciple must continue in His Word

"If ye continue in my word, then ye are my disciples indeed, and ye shall know the truth, and the truth shall make you free" (Jn 8:31-32). Continuing in God's Word suggests a consistent interaction with the Word, rather than a sporadic approach of making contact with it only when necessary. In other religions, indoctrination and brainwashing are tools of raising followers, but in Christianity, it is in understanding and doing the Word, because in the written Word is the power of knowledge and understanding.

A disciple must love other disciples

Love is an overarching parameter for following the Lord. This is understandable because the Bible says, "God is love" (1 Jn 4:8). Christ declares, "By this shall all men know that ye are my disciples, if ye have love one to another" (Jn 13:35). A disciple must be committed to love, especially in those designated areas of love for God, love for neighbor, and love for brothers and sisters in Christ. This is the kind of love that could attract unbelievers by making them want to belong to the environment of love. John, the beloved who is believed to be the closest to Jesus dedicates most of His epistles to the theme of love. No doubt, love is at the core of the practical dissemination of the gospel of Christ. Thus, the Lord's methodology of discipleship is anchored in love.

A disciple must abide in Christ

"I am the vine, ye are the branches. He that abideth in me, and I in him, the same bringeth forth much fruit: For without me ye can do nothing... Herein is my Father glorified, that ye bear much fruit; so shall ye be my disciples" (Jn 15:7-8). The Master's expectation of every disciple is to produce much fruit and the condition for doing so has been specified as abiding in Jesus, and He abiding in the person. To bear fruit is to demonstrate good works, which is reflective of the good and abundant life that Jesus came to give us. In His earthly ministry, Jesus "went about doing good, and healing all that were oppressed of the devil." It is when we produce fruit that God is glorified. The theology of connectivity is the central theme of the Lord's position here. Indeed, what this parameter has shown is what separates Christianity from many other religions of the world. Here the Master sees Himself as the vine, while His followers are branches.

The understanding of this imagery is that both disciples and the Master provide responsorial covering for each other. There cannot be branches without a vine. At the same time, a vine without branches ceases to be a vine. At the very best, it is a stump without any value to the environment in which it is located. There cannot be any life in it because the science of agronomy teaches that it is on the branches that foliage (leaves) are formed, and it is the leaves that make photosynthesis possible. Without the latter, the tree would die. The Lord evoked this serious metaphor in this passage, which speaks to His humility, embracing His followers as friends and brethren. In other religions, followers and masters are mutually exclusive. Their relationships are distant, and their mode of operation is that of master-servants. This is the exact antithesis of what a believer's relationship is with Christ.

A disciple must be involved in Christ's mission

"Go ye therefore, and make disciples of all nations, baptizing them in the name of the Father, and of the Son, and of the Holy Spirit, teaching them to observe all that I command you; and lo, I am with you always even to the end of the age" (Matt 28:19-20).

This is the statement commonly referred to as the Great Commission. It is the main task of today's church, as it was for the early disciples. The action verb (in the imperative) is to "make disciples." Therefore, any disciple who is not passionate in making disciples is not fit to be a disciple. This is what determines the strength and vibrancy of the church. George Barna wrote, "The strength and influence of the church is wholly dependent upon its commitment to true discipleship. Producing transformed lives and seeing those lives reproduced in others, is a core challenge to believers and the local church."[3]

Definition of a Disciple

Three common principles could be deduced from the above qualifications. These principles are: sacrificial, relational, and transformational. Thus, a clear portrait of a disciple should reflect these principles. Once the picture is clear, it is possible for churches to know whether they are making true disciples or not. By definition therefore, *a disciple is someone who, having accepted the saving grace of Jesus Christ is determined to surrender his life to Christ, and live fully for Him in every aspect of his/her life. This individual must be committed to discover and develop his or her gifts and abilities, and deploy them fully for the service of Christ in an environment of communal love, and for the expansion of God's kingdom.*

With this working definition, it would be relatively easy to establish the benchmark for a disciple, and determine if a church leader is really making disciples or merely building up members, or volunteers.

What Discipleship Is

In the above definition of a disciple, there are some active verbs, which presuppose deliberate but voluntary actions on the part of the subject. These words are: *accept, determine,* and *commit.* The import of these words is that the subject has some deliberate actions to take for certain anticipated outcomes. For instance, he must *accept* his salvation as a condition for his *determination* to live fully for Christ; which precipitates his *commitment* to discover his potential and gifts. This is also conditional to his determination to deploy his talent, and gifts for Christ's mission. What this shows is that discipleship is a process towards a specific goal. Therefore, as discipleship takes place it leads to some specific results. It is an intentional developmental process. George Barna describes the process as "being and reproducing spiritually mature zealots for Christ."[4] Therefore, the intentional process is aimed at making mature, complete and competent followers of Christ.

Jesus knew that as the disciples followed and interacted with Him, they would be transformed into people of a particular lifestyle, who would be like Him in their thoughts, words and actions. There is no doubt that as the disciples interacted with Jesus for three years, they had some identifiable character traits. The transformation was so glaring that the Jerusalem community who knew these men before could see the transformation in them. The Bible records, "Now when they saw the boldness of Peter and John, and perceived that they were unlearned and ignorant men, they marveled; and they took knowledge of them that they had been with Jesus" (Acts 4:13). In Antioch, "The disciples were called *Christians* first" (Acts 11:26). (*Christianos)*, "Follower of Christ," (Strong's G5546).

If the early disciples so imbibed the teaching and character of Jesus that they were noticeable in their communities as changed men, who positively influenced their community, the pertinent question is why the Christians of today are not having the same identification mode that could make them stand out in their communities from unbelievers and as community transformers? This could be due to the kind of disciples the church is making, who have no clear and distinct features. This is also an indication that the process of discipleship and the models are faulty, and therefore, ineffective.

In the quest for a working definition of discipleship in this book, certain principles should be established, which are expected to lead directly to an understanding of the process of disciple making. First, a disciple is made as he is taught the principles of kingdom life. Christ declares, "Seek ye first the kingdom of God and its righteousness, and all these things shall be added unto you" (Matt 6:33). The focus of a disciple is the kingdom of God with its righteousness.

Second, a disciple is made as he is taught to obey God's Law and Commandments, which Jesus has streamlined into two laws: love for God, and love for neighbors. He says, "Thou shall love the Lord your God with all your heart, with all your soul, and with all your mind; and thou shall love thy neighbor as thyself" (Matt 22:37), Love is the basis of a disciple's interaction.

Third, a disciple is made as he is taught how to

represent God in the world. "As my father has sent me, even so send I you" (Jn 20:21). As Jesus came to the world to represent the Father, so has Jesus sent us to the world to represent Him, and impact it for God. This shows that it is the disciple who should be the influencer of his community and not the other way round. It is because the church is not producing true disciples that the society seems to be impacting the church negatively.

Fourth, a disciple is made as he is trained to have the heart of a servant as evident in the following Scripture,

> *Ye know that the princes of the Gentiles exercise exercise authority upon them. But it shall not be so among you; but whosoever will be great among you, let him be your master, and whosoever will be chief among you, let him be our servant; Even as the Son of man came not to be ministered unto, but to minister, and to give his life a ransom for many (Matt 20: 25-28).*

The leadership model propounded by Jesus in His teachings is antithetical to the common understanding of leadership. While Jesus' model emphasizes selfless service, the secular model emphasizes status, benefits of position, and attractions of office. Therefore, anyone who wants to be a disciple must learn to serve, in the same way that Jesus came to "serve and give his life a ransom for many" (Mk 10:45).

Finally, a disciple is made as he is taught how to reproduce himself. It was for this reason that Paul wrote, "And the things that thou hast heard of me among many witnesses, the same commit to faithful men, who shall be able to teach others also" (2 Tim 2:2). This process guarantees continuity and gives life and vibrancy to the church. Therefore, any disciple who is not taught to reproduce himself/herself cannot be a true disciple. As stated by Gordon Ferguson, "Discipling others is the process by which a Christian with a life worth emulating commits himself for an extended period of time to a few individuals who have been won to Christ, the purpose being to aid and guide their growth to maturity and equip them to reproduce themselves in a third generation."[5]

Based on the above guidelines, and the fact that discipleship is an intentional act, which involves a process, a working definition is quite probable. Thus discipleship could be defined as *the process of nurturing a follower of Christ to maturity, helping him/her to discover and develop their gifts and potential for mission, and for reproducing themselves in others, and for the expansion of God's kingdom.*

This is the working definition in the context of this book. The definition is appropriate because it embraces the principles established above, and it also resonates with the following points: First, it is a process that has no terminal point because growing in the image of Christ is a life-long task. Paul wrote, "until we all reach unity in the faith and in the knowledge of the Son of God and become mature, attaining to the whole measure of the fullness of Christ" (Eph 4:13).

Second, the definition is non-discriminatory as it recognizes every person as having the necessary gifts and potential to be developed. Therefore, when the church keeps part of its congregation on the pew, they are keeping potential disciples and leaders as spectators in the church. The consequence is that the church suffers, and Christ's mission of reaching the world also suffers.

Third, one way of determining the effectiveness of discipleship is through the fruit they produce. The Bible says, "By their fruits, ye shall know them" (Matt 7:16). The fruit is produced when the disciple operates in full maturity, and is able to influence the society positively with good works. Jesus taught, "Let your light so shine before men, that they may see your good works, and glorify your Father which is in heaven" (Matt 5:16). Therefore, a true disciple is expected to produce other disciples because it is the nature of the plant that determines the fruit it will produce. Principles of fruitfulness will be discussed in detail in Chapter seven.

CHAPTER 3

Leadership

In the previous chapter, I argued that discipleship is a deliberate process, which requires a deliberate action for its success. This proposition assumes that disciples do not just grow, they are made. They are made within a supportive structure, and with a strategic methodology. Thus, discipleship is a well-thought out process of transforming first time guests in the church to disciples and leaders within a sustainable structure, This is why any disciple produced in a haphazard and unstructured system is very likely to end up as ineffective and unproductive. In this chapter, I intend to discuss the structure and methodology of developing disciples into leadership positions.

A corollary is found in Jim Collins' research findings of how some companies stand out of the pack as they transform from "good to great" companies, and perpetuate their position for years.[1] Although, Jim Collins had his focus on corporate business outfits, the principles established are equally applicable to any organization that aspires to greatness, including the church. Here are some of the principles of "good to great" companies as they are applicable in the church content.

First, leadership stands out as one of the factors responsible for the transformation of the companies. According to Collins, "There are seemingly ordinary people quietly producing extra-ordinary results."[2] He tagged them as "Level 5 Leaders."[3] This description fits the identity of Jesus' disciples, who after they had walked with Jesus for three years, people saw their transformation, and "knowing them as unlearned and ignorant men "they took knowledge of them that they had been with Jesus" (Acts 4:13).

As it was with the early disciples, so it is supposed to be with Jesus' disciples of today. As already emphasized, every member of the church is a potential leader because the Bible confirms that every person has been endowed with gifts, which if discovered and developed could transform an ordinary believer to an extra-ordinary person. This is exactly what leadership is all about, and which I intend to highlight in this chapter.

Second, structure is another identifiable feature of a great organization. Collins discovered that "getting the right people in the right seats would make the leaders able to take the company to somewhere great."[4] When this concept is interpolated into the church context, one could see that the church's transformation to greatness is a factor of its structure. This is why any church which has no sustainable structure for developing its members can hardly experience any meaningful growth.

Third, people are identified as catalysts for growth. Collins found out that "if you have the right people on the bus, the problem of how to motivate and manage people largely goes away."[5] He continues, "Great vision without great people is irrelevant."[6] It seems that the church is adopting a contrary approach by making the congregation run with the church leader's vision, not minding the quality of the members, or whether the members have anything to contribute towards the success of the vision. Still identifying people as the most important asset in an organization, Collins qualifies the ambiguity and relative truthfulness of this assertion by saying, "People are your most important assets turns out to be wrong. People are not your most important assets. The right people are."[7]

Although, not every member is the *right* person by church's standard, yet it is the leader's responsibility to make them right by developing them into leaders who do not need to be tightly managed in running with the church's vision. Thus, in the church context, Collins' assertion could be reframed, still retaining its original meaning by saying that it is not ordinary members that make the church grow; it is members developed into disciples and leaders that make the difference. This is the picture modeled in Jesus' disciples, and which is expected to be modeled in today's church.

The Identity of a Leader

It is necessary, at this point, to identify who a leader is, and the qualities a leader should possess so that a leader would be identifiable wherever one emerges. When the church is able to identify who a leader is, it would be easy for them to set up structures and methods of producing them. Leadership is central to administrative efficacy--whether secular or ecclesiastical. This understanding is essential because of the common connotation of who a leader is supposed to be. Usually, a leader is assumed to be someone at the top echelon of an organization, directing its affairs. When this concept is applied to a church setup, there is only one place reserved for a leader, and that is the position of the overseer/pastor of the church. Such an understanding could be misleading as it cannot be biblically sustained, nor does it lend itself to any practical application, even in secular organizations.

The biblical example of Samuel's anointing of David will make this point clearer. When Samuel saw David's brother, Samuel was attracted to him by his physic and stature. However, God restrained Samuel from anointing him because, "the Lord seeth not as man seeth; for man looketh on the outward appearance, but the Lord looketh on the heart" (1 Sam 16:7). In this instance, the leader God had in mind, contrary to people's choice, was the youngest in the family who was at that particular time in the wilderness keeping their father's sheep. By the culture of that time, it is the first born that occupies a position of prominence in the family. All other siblings have no place, talk less of the last born. However, with God, a leader is not necessarily the most privileged, most talented, or the most skilled because God does not determine a leader based on qualities that appeal to man's criteria. This is why David was described as a man after God's own heart.

Jesus' notion of leadership expressed in His teachings is of the same concept. For instance, Jesus taught that whoever wants to be a leader shall be the servant of all. In other words, a leader is a servant, and anyone who has no heart of service is not fit to be a leader. This notion of leadership is contrary to the secular understanding, where a leader is identified by position, title, responsibilities, and benefits of office.

Therefore, Jesus' idea of leadership is relevant in the church context because it emphasizes service over personal gains and benefits. It then follows that anyone could be a leader once he/she has the heart of service. John Maxwell, a renowned authority in Christian leadership, noted that "all of us are leading in some area, while in other areas, we are being led. No one is excluded from being a leader or a follower."[8] Similarly, James Kouzes and Barry Posner, express rather bluntly, that "leadership is anyone's business"[9] Therefore, with this basic concept of a leader, it is safe to consider every church member as a potential leader who could be developed in the relevant areas of their gifts and strength.

Defining a Leader

There are as many definitions and understanding of a leader as there are books, concepts, and opinions on the subject. The wide parameter already established that everyone is a potential leader makes it expedient for the clarification to be made as to who a true leader is. For instance, Kouzes and Posner in their approach, which appears like their avoidance of a clear-cut definition, saw leaders everywhere they looked. According to them, "Leaders reside in every city, in every position and place. They are employees and volunteers, young and old, rich and poor, male and female. Leadership knows no racial or religious bounds, no ethnic or cultural borders."[10] Maxwell, however, distinguished a leader by the influence he exerts. He opined, "In any given situation with any given group there is a prominent influence." Thus, for him, a leader is "the person others will gladly and confidently follow."[11] Another author, Paul Powell agrees with Maxwell. He states, "The simplest definition of leadership I know is 'influence';" and explains, "It is the ability of one person to influence others to his point of view."[12]

Therefore, the working definition of a leader, in the context of this book is, *someone who has surrendered his life to Christ, and has chosen to serve in the body of Christ, as he/she influences others to bring out the best in them for the service of Christ, and the fulfillment of their life purpose in God's service.*

The Essential Qualities of a Leader

The above definition assumes a leader as person of influence who is supposed to possess some qualities which, are essential to enable him/her carry out their responsibilities. In what follows, I will specify these qualities for the purpose of establishing a standard for the kind of leader the church is expected to develop. The qualities are specifically based on biblical parameters, buttressed by opinions of some notable authors and authorities on the subject:

1. Integrity. A leader must be someone of integrity. In setting out the qualifications for a leader (pastor), Paul wrote to Timothy, "A bishop then must be above reproach" (1 Tim 3:2). He further states, "He must have a good report of them which are without." This means that a leader must be a person of integrity, even by unbelievers' assessment of him. In other words, what attracts people to a leader and makes them give him their loyalty should be the leader's integrity.

In their writing on the subject of integrity, which they referred to as "credibility," Kouzes and Posner tagged it "The first law of leadership."[13] According to them, "Credibility is the foundation of leadership. If people don't believe in the messenger, they won't believe the message."[14] Therefore, a leader of integrity has his words match up with his actions. Maxwell agrees, "For a leader to have the authority to lead, he needs more than the title on his door. He has to have the trust of those who are following him."[15]

2. Spirituality. A leader must be spiritual. As one of the conditions for filling the position of a deacon, the early church specified that the person must be "full of the Holy Spirit" (Acts 6:3). This means that he should be a person who continually yields to the dictate of the Holy Spirit in his/her decision making process. Also, to be spirit-filled must be evident in the person's words and deeds. In other words, a leader is expected to have the fruit of the Spirit-- not some or a fraction of it, but all of it. This is why the bible referred to it as "fruit," a singular formation, and not "fruits" in the plural form.

3. Responsibility. A leader must be responsible. Part of the definition of a leader established in this book is someone who has surrendered his/her life to Christ, and has chosen to serve. Thus, when a leader decides to serve, he/she must be ready to take responsibility for the success or failure of the venture. Collins puts this notion in the most visual way, "A leader looks out the window to apportion credit to factors outside himself when things go well. At the same time, they look in the mirror to apportion responsibility, never blaming bad luck when things go poorly.[16] Harry Truman, a former President of America was quoted by Collins to have said, "You can accomplish anything in life, provided that you do not mind who gets the credit."

A biblical example of responsibility with courage and determination is in the experience of Prophet Isaiah who was called by God to speak an unpopular message. Yet, he did not back away from it, but accepted responsibility by responding to the call, "Here I am! Send me" (Isa 6:8). This is the demonstration of responsibility at its best.

4. Permanent Learner. A leader must be a permanent learner. He/she should not think of having arrived, or being a repository of knowledge. Paul demonstrated this quality when he says, "I press toward the mark for the prize of the high calling of God in Christ Jesus" (Phil 3:14). Any time the followers seem to know more than the leader, the leader's position is being compromised, and his/her effectiveness becomes doubtful.

5. Humility. A leader must be humble, which the leader demonstrates when he/she thinks soberly and appropriately about himself or herself. Paul, in his epistle to the Romans writes, "for I say,... to every man that is among you, not to think of himself more highly than he ought to think; but to think soberly, according as God hath dealt to every man the measure of faith" (Rom 12:3). Humility is one of God's laws of promotion. The Bible says, "Humble yourself therefore, under the mighty hand of God that he may exalt you in due time" (1 Pet 5:6).

This injunction is in conformity with the model of Jesus' teaching on leadership when He says, "Whosoever will be great among you will be your minister; and whosoever of you will be the chiefest, shall be servant of all" (Mk 10:43). Giving his mission to the earth as an example of service in humility, Jesus says, "For the Son of man came not to be ministered unto, but to minister, and to give his life a ransom for many" (Mk 10:45). Kouzes and Posner attest to this truth when they wrote, "But the only way to make a real difference is to do humbly, without regard for recognition, ego, pride, even self-preservation. Of course, Christ is our ultimate example of this kind of humility."[17]

6. Ability. A leader must have the ability to lead. Leadership involves having the ability to get the job done. One of the four reasons Maxwell identified as the cause of failed leadership is, "They do not know how to do it."[18] Moses' father-in-law also used this quality when he advised Moses to select those people he should delegate some of his responsibilities to. He says, "Moreover, thou shalt provide out of all people *able men*... and place such over them, to be rulers of thousands, and rulers of hundreds, rulers of fifties, and rulers of ten" (Ex 18:21, emphasis added). This is a confirmation that at every level of leadership, ability is required.

7. Positivity. A leader must be positive. A leader must have a positive mindset, which is a requirement for cultivating faith and for success. Paul is an example of someone with a positive mindset. He says in one of his writings, "I can do all things through Christ who strengtheneth me" (Phil 4:13). With this kind of attitude, there is no mountain too big that cannot be surmounted because such an attitude can turn problems into blessings. It also has a double-edged effect because attitude is contagious. As it works favorably with the leader, so also it is expected to reflect positively on the followers. A biblical example is Nehemiah's positive attitude to get the wall of Jerusalem built which turned out to be the motivation for the builders. The Bible states,

> *Then said I unto them, ye see the distress that we are in, how Jerusalem lieth waste, and the gates thereof are burnt with fire; come, and let us build up the wall of Jerusalem, that we be no more a reproach. Then I told them of the hand of God which was upon me . . . and they said, Let us rise up and build. so they strengthened their hands for this good work (Neh 3: 17-18).*

This is why the discouragement and frustration of the opposition could not stop the work, and the project was successfully completed. Henry Ford, one of the greatest leaders in industry was quoted as saying, "Enthusiasm is the sparkle in your eyes, the swing in your gait, the grip of your hand, the irresistible surge of will and energy to execute your ideas."[19]

8. Maturity. Leadership is not for a novice or an immature, self-centered person. In listing the qualifications for a pastor, Paul identified maturity as a key point. He warns, "Not a novice, lest being puffed up with pride he fall into the condemnation of the devil" (1 tim 3:6). What determines maturity is the leader's ability to grow out of self-centeredness, and be of selfless service to the people. Kouzes and Posner in writing about selfless service said, "The lesson that leadership is a service and that leaders are servants are likely the most significant Christian feelings about the nature of leadership."[20]

Therefore, any leader who is not ready to serve in a position of a servant is not ready to be a leader. In the same vein, when others are discouraged, leaders are never discouraged. "They keep hope alive by recognizing the dedication of others as they get extraordinary things done."[21]

Having defined who a leader is, and the qualities that make up one, it seems the picture of a leader as defined in this book is evolving into its proper perspective. The next logical issue is to focus on the structure under which leadership could be effectively developed. This is a point of great divergence in the church, and the reason why the church is not producing the same kind of leaders. There are as many structures as there are churches and denominations, each of which has its peculiar kind of leaders they produce. The consequence is the church's inability to produce leaders that are designed purposely for fulfilling the divine mandate of making disciples of nations.

CHAPTER 4

Leadership Developmental Structure

Leaders do not just emerge supernaturally; they are made systematically. The fact that they are made makes it expedient for the process to be modeled in some structure. The Bible says, "By their fruit ye shall know them" (Matt 7:16). The fruit is the most positive and empirical identifier of a plant. Therefore, the kind of leaders a church produces speaks to the character and nature of the church that produces it, determined by the structure and methodology through which such leaders are developed. In this section, I will discuss the structure within which leaders are best developed for discipling nations.

As an analogy, a natural plant requires certain environmental conditions like good soil, sunlight, water and air to grow and bear fruits. So also does the development of a leader need to be established in some favorable structure to be optimally effective.

The Small Group Structure

`There are various structures that the church could choose from in developing its leaders. I want to show, with some convincing evidence, what I consider the most favorable structure. Continuing with the analogy of the natural plant, and referring to the parable of the sower, the Bible states that a sower sowed his seed into different kinds of soil by the roadside, among thorns, and on the rock--with predictable negative outcomes. However, the seed sown on the good ground was able to bear fruit, with differing levels of output. The bible says, "But others fell into good ground, and brought forth, some an hundredfold, some sixtyfold, and some thirtyfold" (Matt 13:8). This shows that ecological conditions are predominant factors in the output of the sown seed.

Similarly, different kinds of structures of leadership development would naturally produce different kinds of leaders. As the sower would naturally prefer the environment that yields the optimum level of output, so also a church is expected to adopt the structure of leadership development that would produce the most effective leaders. I wish to identify the small group structure as the model for such maximum level leadership.

This assertion agrees with Dave Earley's observation when he wrote, "Experience shows that leadership development and discipleship happens best in the small group ministry of a local church."[1] He further observed, "The churches experiencing explosive and healthy growth are churches that are raising up disciple-making leaders in their small groups to lead their small groups."[2] It is therefore, evident that the churches that have small group structure have some good outcome to show forth in their experience. Writing on his experience of small groups, Jeffery Arnold says, "Small groups produce multiple benefits. They can release the ministry of the laity, offer superior pastoral care, and better challenge people to be like Jesus Christ."[3]

Arnold identifies three operational foundations for small group ministry. These are sociological, biblical, and theological foundations.[4] He noted that in the American social system, "45 per cent of Americans are in some form of a small group, and many more indicate an interest in joining one group or more groups,"[5] affirming that the small group system is not alien in the American social system. In considering its relevance to the church, Arnold observes, "Of those people in groups, 60 percent are in church-related groups, and a large portion of the remaining 40 percent is studying spiritual issues." He concludes, "These statistics demonstrate that small groups are a powerful force in American culture."[6]

The Basis of Small Group Structure

Arnold's viewpoint is relevant here in establishing the basis for small group structure. Thus, I will consider the sociological, biblical and theological foundations; and the example of the Early church.

Sociological Foundation

Just as the American social system supports the small group structure, so it is with other social systems around the world. For the same reasons, small groups are sociologically beneficial to the church. First, small groups provide a safe place where people can be heard. Second, small groups give any dysfunctional society a positive model for building healthy relationships, especially in the family and in other relationships. Third, people are known deeply in small group settings where they are prayed for, cared for, and challenged in a way that no other church structure can offer. Fourth, small groups can keep people on the cutting edge by consistently demanding more in the way of Christian leadership.[7]

When compared with the regular church situation in which there is no small group structure, but every member is just a face in the crowd, interpersonal relationship is not easily forged. As observed by Leith Anderson, "The small group movement is more than support groups. It is a grass-root movement of people gathering for friendship and common interest."[8] Therefore, small group relationship is expected to provide psychological and sociological satisfaction to those who belong to them.

Biblical Foundation

There are many biblical references in both the Old and New Testaments in support of small group structure.

God blessed Adam and Eve, "Be fruitful and multiply, and replenish the earth and subdue it; and have dominion over the fish of the sea, and over the fowl of the air, and over every living thing that moveth upon the earth" (Gen 1:28). It is evident from this blessing that multiplication—physical and spiritual—was God's intention. It is by their fruitfulness by multiplication that the earth could be filled, replenished, and subdued. The same kind of mandate was reiterated to Noah following the destruction of the earth by flood. "And God blessed Noah and his sons, and said unto them, be fruitful and multiply, and replenish the earth" (Gen 9:1).

God called Abraham, saying "get thee out of thy country, and from thy kindred, and from thy father's house, unto a land that I will show thee" (Gen 12:1). God's intention was to make him *a great nation*. Though, Abraham was yet to have a child, God still promised to *multiply him exceedingly*. Some centuries later, when Abraham's descendants were being led as God's people into the land of Canaan, God gave them the Law; and in the process, confirms the divine blessing once again, "So I will turn toward you and make you fruitful and multiply you, and I will confirm my covenant with you" (Lev 26:9).

Theological Foundation

Jesus modeled His ministry on small groups. He chose twelve men to follow Him, with the sole intention of *making them fishers of men*. This is why Jesus spent most of His time with the disciples. "They were together constantly; they travelled together, shared meals, experienced mutual hardship, and literally lived together."[9] Thus, the small group structure was the leadership training method that Jesus used in developing the disciples. His goal was to equip them in such a way that they would continue to carry on the work of the gospel after He would have returned to heaven. With the kind of interaction that was evident between Jesus' and His disciples, Jesus was building with them relationship, and not an institution.

The basic point here is that if Jesus could model His ministry on small groups, there is no reason why the church should not follow the same model. If we are to be imitators of Christ, this is an aspect of Jesus' ministry the church should imitate. This is not just for the purpose of being Christ-like (which is expected of us), but also because of the indisputable success of such a model. It is the effectiveness of the small group structure that made the disciples able to carry the gospel from "Jerusalem, unto Judea, to Samaria, and to the uttermost part of the earth" (Acts 1:8). Therefore, for the present church to witness beyond our immediate community, and make some impact on our society and nation, we should adopt the model of small groups as Jesus also operated in the small group model.

Here is the point: Christianity flourishes in relationships—personal relationship with God, relationship with neighbors, and relationship with fellow believers. This is the summation of the Great Commandment, and the New Commandment. Relationship is the reason behind God's intention for creating mankind, whom He intended for fellowship and for His pleasure. Fellowship with God was a regular and normal thing with Adam and Eve, until the devil threw a spanner in their wheel of relationship by leading them into sin. Yet, God in His mercy made alternative provision for restoring man's fellowship with Him through Jesus' redemptive sacrifice on the Cross.

Example of the Early Church

As earlier stated in the previous chapter, the early church was established on small group structure, which had its natural elements in the home. This is because the home was the social basis of interaction for the family and community. Thus, in conformity with this social phenomenon, the early church used to meet in houses. For example, the Scripture identifies the churches that met in the homes of Priscilla and Aquila, and Philemon. In addition, the Scripture gives a glimpse of the functioning of such house churches,

> *And they continued steadfastly in the apostles' doctrine and fellowship, and in breaking of bread, and in prayers. And fear came upon every soul: and many wonders and signs were done by the apostles. And all that believed were together, and had all things common; And sold*

their possessions and goods, and parted them
to all men as every man had need. And they,
continuing daily with one accord in the temple,
and breaking bread from house to house, did eat
their meat with gladness and singleness of
heart, Praising God, and having favor with all the
people. And the Lord added to the church daily
such as should be saved (Acts 2: 42-47, emphasis
added).

There are some common practices by the early church in this passage that shows their communality and closeness with one another. Therefore, it can safely be concluded that "meetings in homes provided the backbone of the church structure."[10] McBride observed that the house church remained the most pervasive form of church structure up until the time of Emperor Constantine (274-337 AD), when church buildings began to replace the house church.[11] From this time on to the present, the erroneous perception of the church being referred to as a building rather than the Body of Christ emerged. This concept shall be discussed in greater details in chapter five.

The exponential growth which the early church experienced, could be traceable to its small group structure. For example, the Bible says, "And in those days, when the number of the disciples was *multiplied*." (Acts 6:1, emphasis added). In the same account, it was reported, "The number of the disciples *multiplied* in

Jerusalem" (Acts 6:7), emphasis added). There is a significant difference between *multiply* and *increase*. Multiplication indicates an exponential increase rather than normal increase. Yonggi Cho explains this point from the standpoint of the cells in the human body. He writes,

> The church is a living organism, and cell groups are living cells, and they function like the cells in the human body. In a living organism, the cells grow and divide. Where once there was one cell, there become two. They become four, then eight, then sixteen, and so on. Cells don't simply add to the body, they are multiplied by geometric progression."[12]

Thus, the church is not to be satisfied with normal increase contrary to the practice of some churches that celebrate a couple of families' visit to the church as first timers.

In every aspect of Christian doctrine therefore, relationship is the focus, and the church leader has the responsibility of promoting the relationship of their members with God, with neighbors, and other believers for their spiritual vibrancy.

Cell Group Models

There are different models of small groups. For clarification, let us look at some of the models as categorized by Joel Comiskey, as he considered them from the process of their pragmatic evolvement and growth as movements. He identified the following: the Korean Cell-church movement, the Meta Model, the Pure, Pure Cell church, the G12 phenomenon, and the Radical Middle.[13]

The Korean Cell-Church Movement

This movement, which was led by David Yonggi Cho, started in his church in Seoul, South Korea in 1984, and through this model, his church was transformed into the largest church in the world with over 500,000 worshippers. Although, many church leaders tried to transfer the model to the American system, Comiskey observes, "Majority who tried to repeat Cho's small-group system failed."[14] He attributed the reason for their failure as Cho's inability to give "the nuts and bolts of making the system work in his books."[15] However, many still regard the model as the foremost of the models, which has opened the eyes of church leaders to church growth through home cell groups.

The Meta Model

The adoption of Cho's model in the American culture was traced to Carl George who demonstrates that "the church of the future would be a collection of small groups."[16] He coined "Meta" for his model[17]. In this model, George regarded Sunday school classes, ministry teams, outreach teams, worship production team, sports teams, recovery groups, and others as small groups. By this all-embracing approach to small groups, churches regarded themselves as already having small groups, but because there was no concrete approach to developing leaders, "the quality control of the cell itself suffered under the meta model."[18]

The Pure, Pure Cell church

This model, developed by Ralph Neighbor appeared in 1990. The main emphasis is on equipping every cell member for cell-based evangelism. Neighbor detailed the process of equipping every cell member for the work of ministry, especially evangelism.[19] The awareness which this movement created did not last for long because of the impression which church leaders had in Neighbor's approach that he was "against the conventional church in tone and operation."[20]

The G12 Phenomenon

This model is traceable to the International Charismatic Mission (ICM) in Bogota, Columbia, initiated in the 1990's. Although, the model has its origin in Cho's model, it was given a cultural twist that made the model adaptable. By the application of this system, it was reported that ICM grew into multiple thousands.[21] This model regarded everyone as a potential cell leader; and established a "clear, dynamic equipping training track that prepared everyone for ministry."[22] Following Jesus' example of twelve disciples, this model encourages the multiplication of a group as it gets as large as twelve members, with the new group to be led by a trained apprentice. This model promotes a healthy growth of the church as every member is recognized as a potential leader is assisted to develop his/her gifts for ministry work.

The Radical Middle

This model seems to have Comiskey's sympathy and inclination. According to him, leaders in this group "greatly desire to maintain the key components of cell ministry, but they are just as passionate to make sure it actually works in North America."[23] Exploring the term, "Radical Middle," Comiskey says, it "highlights the radical nature of cell ministry yet also proclaims the need for practicality—it must work."[24] This presupposes that this group cannot be identified with a specific model, or a coaching structure. Their approach is "if it works, use it. If it doesn't work, don't."[25] They are open to adopting principles that make cell groups work in other churches and applying it to their own system in as much as it is able to satisfy their motive, which is "to make disciples, develop leaders, evangelize more effectively, and eventually plant new cell churches."[26]

Although, this broad categorization is not able to define churches in terms of the operation of their small groups, it gives us some necessary information as to how these groups evolved, and how any church or individual could be led into operating small groups of whatever structure suits their purpose and culture.

Strategy for Effective Leadership Development

So far, I have tried to establish the basis for leadership development as small group structure. However, it is not enough to set up the structure without an understanding of the methodology of the structure for leadership development. In concluding this section therefore, I intend to set up a methodology for the development of leaders. This is necessary because in Jesus' divine mandate to the church, He mentioned the method by which the nations could be discipled. He says, "Teaching them to observe all things whatsoever I have commanded you" (Matt 28:20).

What method of teaching did Jesus have in mind? It is clear that the method is teaching by observation. What are they to observe? They are to observe Jesus' teaching and instructions. My intention here is to expatiate on how believers could internalize the observatory mode of teaching in their relationships in a small group structure as they reflect on teachings and Laws as the Great Commandment, and the New Commandment.

It is interesting to note that *to observe* in Greek is *tereo*, which means *keep*, or *keep watch*. In a broad sense, it means, *Give attention to.*[27] Within the church setting, it is difficult for members to watch or give attention to whatever goes on in a two-hour weekly service in a participatory and involving way. Rather, the congregation is made to watch in a passive and non-involving way. Therefore, in a regular church setting, it is difficult for members to accomplish fully what Jesus has commanded the church to teach. This is Yonggi Cho's point of emphasis when he writes, "While they are having words of encouragement from the pulpit, they are experiencing in church much the same thing as in secular life. They are merely spectators."[28]

However, with small groups, it is a different platform. Cho observes, "Home cell groups provide a real opportunity for people to find meaningful involvement in the life of their church... there is an opportunity for everybody to become involved."[29] The way it works is that in small groups, "members have the opportunity to bring a word of prophecy, tongues, and interpretation, a word of knowledge or a word of wisdom. Each member can pray for the sick, and in faith believe God will hear his prayer and heal the sick."[30]

The point is that the teaching methodology that involves observation and keeping watch with the intention of learning by example is better done in a small group setting because small groups provide the effective setting that could facilitate human interaction and relationships. Let us look at the applicability of this method of teaching in imparting the lessons of the Great Commandment and the New Commandment.

The Methodology

The Great Commandment

According to Jesus, the first and great commandment to Christians is to love God with all their heart, soul, and mind; while the second is like it, which is to love their neighbors as themselves (Matt 22: 37-39). The content of this kind of teaching is love, which incidentally, is demonstrable by action. When a person shows love by action, others are able to observe and replicate it. For example, when a member is celebrating his/her anniversary or success in his/her career, other members show their joy as they celebrate with that member. The same is true of any member who is mourning the loss of a loved one, the group rally around the member to commiserate with him/her. This is in line with the biblical injunction that says, "Rejoice with them that do rejoice, and weep with them that weep" (Rom 12:15).

There are some small groups that would not want to see the child of a member being sent out of school for the parents' inability to pay the child's school fees. In expressing love, some members would go out of their way to support this family by helping to offset the child's school fees. This is love by action, and when love is expressed in this way, it becomes a lifestyle of the group as other members would replicate the same actions whenever another member needs any form of help from the group.

The New Commandment

Jesus says,

"A new commandment I give unto you, that ye love one another, as I have loved you, that ye also love one another. By this shall all men know that ye are my disciples, if ye love one another" (Jn 13:34-35).

In this Scripture, Jesus gave believers the standard of love that He wants them to demonstrate to one another, and that standard is the kind that Jesus showed when He gave His life for us. This is what is referred to as *sacrificial love*. This is the kind of love that you show without expecting anything in return, no matter the cost to you.

Anywhere this kind of love is demonstrated, it is evident that the people are disciples of Christ. "By this shall all men know that ye are my disciples" Jn 13:35). When unbelievers observe this kind of love, they would want to belong because such love is not common, and since everyone wants to be loved, they are drawn into such a group where love is easily expressed without any strings attached.

Stanley and Bill Willits, writing on their experience of small groups have this to say, "We have found that people are naturally cared for best by those who know them best—those with whom they are walking through life."[31] Thus, the small group structure provides such an intimate environment that is difficult to find in other relationships. Yonggi Cho gives a glimpse of what he observed in his church's small groups when he writes,

> "There are often tears when friends have to separate to attend different meetings. There is much security for the members in the cell groups. Such one becomes a family member with the others of the group in a kind of community relationship, which is more than community. The fellowship goes beyond counsel and prayer; members really take care of one another."[32]

The fact that small group operation is not limited to Sunday worship service, but extends to other days of the week when groups meet in their homes makes this methodology practicable and effective, not forgetting the relaxed atmosphere of the home. These and other factors make small groups meeting in homes an effective tool for individual growth and development.

The next Chapter takes readers into the research methodology and findings. I suggest you skip Chapter 5 if you are not research inclined.

CHAPTER 5

The Church's Empirical Growth Pattern

In this Chapter, I will look at the church in its empirical form to determine how it operates in its dynamics and structure in determining how effective the institution is in its responsibility of discipling nations. The research which was conducted among some selected churches in America would be analyzed in determining the church's position and effectiveness in the determined factors of the church's growth rate, the church's vision, training and development programs, soul-winning programs, and small group structures. How have these factors influenced the health and growth of the church?

.

The Church

The logical starting point is to have a clear understanding of what a church really means. This is necessary because having a biblical concept of the church in mind would clear any form of misconception and misunderstanding of the concept. What is the biblical connotation of a church? The church, (*ekklesia* in Greek), in a general sense means "people of God in congregation."[1] The same word *ekklesia* is used in Pauline epistles to refer to church as *the Body of Christ*. The word *ekklesia* literally refers to church as the *called (kaleo) out (ek)* ones. This means that the church is *called out* from the world by God and 'called out' to proclaim His greatness.

Elmer Towns and Ed Stetzer identified the following features of a New Testament church.[2] First, a church is a group of people that covenants together. This is to say a group is not a church until they demonstrate a spiritually binding union with one another in the bonds of faith. Second, it is a group that maintains certain biblical practices like baptism and the Lord's Supper. These are the well codified, voluntarily or involuntarily practices of a New Testament church.

Third, a church is a group, which presents the Word of God in preaching and teaching. An essential tenet of the operational pedagogy of a Christian Church is to emulate some aspects of the modes of operation of its Master, Jesus Christ, who was known for preaching, teaching, and healing. Preaching and teaching are the two modes and strategies for which the word of God is disseminated.

Fourth, a church is a group that is served by two types of leaders: pastors (elders) and deacons. The laity and the clergy are two componential constituencies in any definable New Testament Church. The clergy, paid or unpaid, often comprises of pastors (elders), and deacons.

Though, their designations may vary from denomination to denomination, this is essentially the common model of Church leadership.

By this clarification, a church is better understood as a group of people, rather than a building neither does a church need a building to be called a church. Therefore, it is not necessarily, where a church meets that qualifies it as a church, but when a group of worshippers meets the biblical specifications enumerated above, the group qualifies as a church.

Summary of Research Sampling

In the survey, different churches in a variety of sizes, ranging from congregations of 50 to 2500, and in different locations were sampled. For example, I gathered data from six churches in Atlanta, Georgia, a multicultural metropolitan city; four churches in Madison, Wisconsin, a middle-level semi-urban city; four churches in Chicago, Illinois, a cosmopolitan mega city; two churches in Nashville, Tennessee, a mid-level urban community; and four churches in New York, a cosmopolitan multicultural mega city. The length of service of the pastors in-charge of these churches range from three to twenty-seven years.

These samples are randomly selected, but they are wide enough to give a fair representation of the American churches in particular, and the body of Christ in general. In all, twenty respondents were sampled, and the churches are identified numbers that were randomly ascribed to them and the numbers are maintained throughout the research. The goal is to conceal the respondents' identities and keep them as anonymous as legally and morally feasible. Similarly, pastors' names are not disclosed for the same reason.

The analysis shows a clear representation of what the churches have entered in their responses to the survey questionnaire. All analyses are based on scholarly speculations and not meant to be a prophetic pronouncement on any of the churches surveyed. The factors considered in this chapter in speculating on the health of the churches are the following: church's growth rate, vision, training and development structure, soul-winning methods, and small group structures.

Church's Retention and Growth Rate

In determining the church's growth rate, the pastors were asked to enter the average number of first time guests which the churches received in a one month period. This figure is used to determine the number they retained based on the retention ratio which the pastors have indicated in their questionnaire. The outcome determines how effective the churches are in converting their guests who are also their new converts and trainees into discipleship. It is when the church is able to retain the new converts that they would be able to train them, and help them discover their gifts.

Although, it is not everyone who is retained by the church that would eventually be a true disciple, for the purpose of this analysis, the assumption is that all the retained converts were trained for discipleship. The retention rate computed in this section will be used as the standard rate for all the factors of church health considered.

Summary

In the churches' attraction rate of first time guests, the following observations were made:

- 12 churches (60%) attract an average of 5 guests each in a one-month period.
- 6 churches (30%) attract an average of 15 guests each within the same time frame.
- 2 churches (10%) attract more than 60 guests within the same time frame.
- Collectively all the churches attract 300 guests within the same time frame.

Retention Rate

Out of the total number of guests attracted, the churches' retention rates are as follows:

- The 12 churches that attract an average of 5 guests each retain a total of 10.5 of the guests = an average of 1 guest per church per month.
- The 6 churches that attract an average of 15 guests each are able to retain a total of 19.5 guests = an average of 4 guests per church per month.

- The 2 churches that attract an average of 60 guests each retain a total of 51 guests = an average of 25 guests per church per month.
- Out of the total number of 300 guests for all the churches, only 83.5 were retained = 28%.

Comments

At the rate of 28 percent of retaining and discipling converts, it is obvious that churches are not growing at the rate at which they can disciple all nations effectively. This is a confirmation that the churches' strategy and methods of evangelism and discipleship are not effective, compared with the biblical standard of the early church in which "the Lord added to the church daily such as should be saved." This is also a confirmation that the strategy, which could make the churches grow exponentially, is not yet discovered or implemented.

Effect of Church Vision on Church Health

Vision is an important aspect of church health, but more importantly is a clear and concise vision. It is one thing to have a clear vision, it is another thing to inspire the vision in the congregation because Christianity is not a lone journey; it is a group activity. Dale Earley quoted the church researcher and author, George Barna as saying, "Let's get one thing straight from the start. If you want to be a leader, vision is not an option; it is part of the standard equipment of a real leader." He continues,

"The equitation is quite simple, no vision = no leadership."[3]

Discussion

Churches 6 and 12 have no vision statement. It is assumed that by not indicating a vision statement, they have none. By not having a vision statement, such churches are probably following the status quo and therefore, cannot actively engage their members and consequently cannot grow. This kind of church would eventually extinct. This is not a surprising outcome because the bible has already warned that "Where there is no vision, the people perish" (Prov 29:18). It is also not a surprise that Church Six which has no vision, also has no catchment area of evangelism, and therefore has zero increase in a one month period.

Church Twelve, which has the "world" as its focus area, and is poised to "build families, and transform communities, reconciling cultures, and impacting the world," is able to have an average of six additional persons in a one-month period. This figure is relatively high probably due to the high number of guests out of which the church claims to retain sixty in a month. However, the retention ratio of ten percent is common as with the other churches surveyed.

Church Two's vision is "to transform lives and transform communities." This does not represent a vision in the true and biblical sense of the word. The question as to what the church is transforming from and to what remains unclear. This is a generic statement, and while generic vision can deal with social issues generally it cannot deal with personal spiritual matters of members.

Many orthodox Churches have traditionally followed such genetic visions, and therefore, if they are able to deal with larger social issues, like the Salvation Army or the Catholic Missions, they would find it difficult to reach individual souls and transform their lives for the service of the Lord. Churches with such indefinably large visions often dwindle in true memberships. Although, the focus area is the community, the church could retain an average of 1.5 persons in a one-month period.

Church Five's vision "to empower and restore families" does not state what to "empower" the families to do, and what to restore it from. This too, like Church Two, provides a generic declaration. It sounds more like a political statement than a vision. Pastors with such vision could only give motivational speeches rather than provide life-changing messages for the congregation. They could talk about "family values," "sanctity of marriage," and many nice sounding social issues. As good as this vision appears, it does not translate to the transformation of the members' heart or their development into true discipleship. The average for first time guests for this church is 15 in a one month period. The increase of 10.5 persons seems relatively high because of the church's claim of 70 percent retention rate.

Church Seven's vision of "carrying out the great commission" is like saying, "I am in school because I want to be a student." Once you are in school, being a student is no more a choice. Similarly, carrying out the great commission is the essence of being a church. However, this church fails to articulate what it needs to do in carrying out the great commission.

Again, it is a sound good "vision" lacking in specificity because it is shortsighted. The limited scope of such vision is manifested in its tendency to get the attention of those who love theological languages such as the phrase, "the great commission," but as soon as they are drawn to such a church and find it to lack in substance, they will not be able to stay there or they could just remain there for socialization rather than for any spiritual benefit. The church averages 2.5 persons increase in a one month period.

Another vaguely stated vision is that of Church Sixteen, which states, "Connecting people to God through Christ." So also is Church Eighteen whose vision, among other things is, "To take our neighbors to heaven." It is difficult to explain this kind of vision to a congregation that is struggling with the concept of heaven. As a result, it would be difficult to get the people understand how the church would get them to a place they probably do not believe exists. For this vision to be meaningful, it has to be explicit by making the people understand where they are presently and what the church intends them to become after connecting them. Again, this is a generic statement and in no way would such vision address or meet the needs of the people. It is not surprising that the churches average one person increase in a one-month period.

Church Eight's vision states, "We preach Christ to our community, help them realize their potential, train them in ministry, and release them to God's work." It would be difficult to share this kind of vision with the congregation because it does not state what the church is to preach; in what kind of community it is to preach it; and the target group it is intended to reach in the community. The inability of the church to attract not more than 0.5 persons is an expected outcome.

Comments

It is not a surprise that the survey findings are exactly as predicted, because the churches either have no vision or have visions that are vague. I observe that church leaders do not seem to understand the essence of vision in carrying out their assignment. It seems that they believe that once they have the necessary gifts as believers, and believe they are called into ministry, vision is of no use. This is why it seems in the survey that, church leaders describe what they aspire to do, rather than what God has given them as assignment to accomplish.

These observations explain the current state of the church health. A leader who has no vision is better not assume the duty of leading a church because he/she is leading the church to an uncertain destination. Every great venture has its starting point in a dream, including what is now known as the largest church in the world. Yonggi Cho, the pastor of the church attest to this fact when he writes, "You are only going to grow only as big as your dream."[4] The low growth rates of churches in this research are a reflection of the absence of a God-inspired visions without which the church has no motivation for growth.

An evidence of growth is fruitfulness which is typified in the context of church growth by the number of churches. As analyzed in the survey, all the churches together are able to plant 14 new churches in a one year period. This is a confirmation that the systems the churches are adopting for their growth is not yielding the required fruit. Whereas, the strategy of small groups makes the evolvement of new churches inevitable, because as the cell groups grow and multiply, new churches are naturally born.

Yonggi Cho, expressed the basis of the growth of his church thus, "Begin to look for needs, loving people and helping them to start a nucleus of a home cell group. As each cell grows and begin to divide, you'll soon have a church."[5] Mike Slaughter warns, "If we are not giving birth to new churches, we will become irrelevant to the next generation."[6] It is therefore, no wonder that the church is fast becoming irrelevant in the present American culture because of its inability to give birth to young churches in their neighborhoods.

Effect of Church's Training & Development Program on Church Health

As it has already been established, training is an important aspect of church growth because successful multiplication will never happen without the development of potential leaders. In this research, the development program of the churches surveyed was determined by asking pastors to ascertain the different levels attainable in their training programs from level 1-5.

Fifteen churches, representing 75 percent of the churches, have some kinds of training programs. Three churches which represent 15 percent of the churches have no training program of any kind. This is also with the understanding that a standard training program is usually more than one level because the first stage is usually what churches generally regard as new member's class. This is like an induction program by which new members are familiarized with the church environment and structure.

Out of the fifteen churches that have programs, four (which represent 20 percent) have the one-level kind of training program. To determine the effectiveness of the churches' training programs based on the anticipated new skills to be acquired by the participants, pastors are asked to determine what their trainees are expected to be skilled in doing after the training. The following options were available: Taking part in church activities, starting his/her ministry, winning souls, training others, and small groups.

All respondents indicated multiple choices except Church Five which trains only for soul-winning, and Churches Seventeen, and Eighteen, which train only for church ministries. Therefore, analyzing each factor for its growth effect could be misleading.

The following results are evident from the survey:

- 90 percent of the churches determine their members' new skills by their taking part in church activities, or belonging to church ministries
- 50 percent determine their members' skills by their ability to win souls
- 40 percent determine their members' skills by their ability to train others
- 35 percent determine their members' skills by their ability to lead small groups
- 15 percent determine their members' skills by their ability to start the ministries of their calling.

Discussion

It is evident from the above result that 90 per cent of the churches surveyed are activity motivated. These are churches that believe that spiritual growth of their members is dependent on the members' involvement in church activities like ushering, choir, teaching Sunday school or children ministry. This could also mean members' commitment to some church ministries like men's and women's fellowship, youth, and prayer groups. In these churches, leaders are developed specifically for church activities and programs.

With 50 percent of churches developing their members for soul winning, it shows that about half of the churches in the country depend on seekers to come into their churches to find salvation rather than their members going outside the four walls of the church to extend salvation to them. This also shows that about half of the churches have no program of making their member soul winners. Thus, it shows that half of the congregations in the church are mere spectators who are in the church just to watch how the pastors and other people perform on a Sunday service. As pointed out in Chapter two, this is an indication of an unhealthy Body of Christ. When half of the congregation is not active in discipling others, it is evident that the body of Christ is hemiplegic (one side paralysis) which makes the whole body ineffective.

A true disciple should be able to train other disciples. In the survey, 40 percent train their members for the purpose of making them trainers. Unless the church makes the conscious effort of producing producers, the church cannot grow. Those who train their members to lead small groups constitute 35 percent of the respondents. What this shows is that the churches do not design their small groups for church growth and members' spiritual development which is a great omission. As a result, they are missing out on the effectiveness of the small group structure which has been proved to be one of the most effective structures for church growth.

The Bible makes it clear that God has given gifts to every member of the Body of Christ; and it is the responsibility of the pastor to help them develop those gifts. However, when only 15 percent of the churches train their members for the purpose of developing and deploying them, it is completely at variance with God's expectation of the church. This shows that pastors are more interested in keeping members purposely for building up the membership of their church, rather than building the Body of Christ for the expansion of God's kingdom.

Summary

Without a clear strategy of developing leaders, the church cannot grow. The process of developing leaders, though very involving, is a worthwhile process, which every church should determine to undertake. Earley, writing about the training of members, states, "It is hard work. And it is worth it. When you know people you've developed are leading healthy, growing, multiplying groups, you'll be glad you paid the price and so will they."[7]

Effect of Church's Soul-winning Methods on Church Health

The basic responsibility of the church is soul winning, and any church which is successful in this responsibility by having steady growth and increase as they utilize the most effective methods of growth also has a healthy church. My intention here is to find out the methods which the churches adopt and how effective they are. The following are the methods listed in the questionnaire: Mass-evangelism (through electronics and print media), door-to-door, crusades/programs/revivals, small groups, existing members, others (to be specified).

These are the pastors' responses:

- One church (Church Six), which represents 5 percent of the respondents has no specific model, with the resultant zero increase in a one-month period.
- Church Twelve, (5%), adopts only one method which is "door to door," and has an average increase of six persons within the same time frame.

All other churches (90%) make use of a combination of 2-5 methods, which makes the effectiveness of each of the methods unpredictable.

- One church (5%) makes use of mass-evangelism method.
- 14 churches, (70%) go door to door; 5 Churches (25%) use program/crusades method
- 12 churches (60%) make use of small groups
- 13 churches (65%) make use of existing members.

Discussion

Mass-evangelism method through electronics and print media is the widest in coverage, and also the most expensive. For 5 percent of the churches to be involved in this method is understandable. It is very likely to be the cost factor, which many of the churches are not able to afford.

Door-to-door method is surprisingly the dominant method as 75 percent of the churches take to it, despite the increasing resentment of the society of this method. This is why it is not yielding the best result. It is therefore, evident that churches keep knocking at doors probably because they have no way of shunning the tradition.

Making use of existing members has some implications. It is the second highest method after door-to-door with 70 percent of the churches, even though only 50 percent of the churches surveyed claimed to train their members for soul-winning. This means that most of the churches which make use of this model do not train their members specifically for this purpose. This is an indication that although churches are aware of the effectiveness of this method, they do not have the training structure that would make it happen. The result is that members are not effective in what they do.

Small groups are not effectively utilized for soul winning as only 60 percent of the churches make use of them. This shows that about two-thirds of the churches make use of what appears to be the most effective method of reaching the greatest number of people, while one-third does not. While churches have the communities as their target areas, they do not seem to have the right method of reaching out to them effectively. The result is a church that lacks steady growth. It is surprising that only 30 percent of the churches organize programs for enticing seekers into the church. This is an indication that churches are getting conscious of the ineffectiveness of this method. This seems to be a healthy diversion from the traditional approach that has been the bane of the church for years.

Comments

The effectiveness of the methods of evangelism adopted by the churches are suspect as the twenty churches surveyed are collectively able to attract 300 guests to their churches in a one month period, and could retain only 83.5 persons, which represents 28 percent performance. This is an indication of the ineffectiveness of the methods of evangelism used by the churches. The combination of these methods leaves a large exit door open, as more people exit from the churches than they come in. This is a leaking system which is typical of almost all the churches, and which is the cause of their decline. It shows that the churches need to adopt a more sustainable and attractive method that could keep new members attracted and connected.

The evangelical efforts of churches are not bringing the desired result because they are not using the right methods, and the members they are using are not well trained for the task. This is why my suggestions in this book becomes relevant as they are intended to proffer what is considered as an effective method, for keeping the church vibrant and members spiritually healthy. It is evident that what drives the churches in their present mode of operation is survival strategy, and evangelism rather than discipleship and group activities. However, with the small group model, it would be possible for churches to develop disciples, and raise leaders who would be able to develop other leaders and keep outsiders attracted and connected.

Effect of Church's Small Groups on Church Health

As ascertained in the previous chapter, small group structure stands out as the most effective for church growth and spiritual edification of members. Henry Clouds and John Townsend attest to this fact when they write, "We've come to believe that small group is without a doubt one of the most powerful tools of life change and spiritual growth."[8] In his own research findings, Comiskey, saw a correlation between his research and what a research finding of 2002 revealed. He discovered,

"Cell churches not only grew faster but were far healthier in every area." In terms of growth, he found out that "cell churches demonstrate an average growth rate almost double that of non-cell churches."[9]

In determining the effectiveness of small groups in this research, the following criteria are specified in the questionnaire as to what the churches make use of their small groups for. The options are: attracting and retaining new members; for evangelism; for members' development; as church ministry groups; as prayer groups; and as community support groups.

Summary

- Sixteen churches (80%) claim to have small groups for new members' class
- Thirteen churches (65%) use small groups for soul winning purposes. Twelve churches (60%) use their small groups for developing members
- Fourteen churches (65%) have ministry groups that function to foster church activities and services
- Twelve churches (60%) have prayer groups, while ten Churches (50%) have support groups.

Discussion

Four churches (Churches Three, Nine, Sixteen, and Twenty) have all the different kinds of small groups and collectively have 45 guests in a one month period, out of whom they are able to retain 6 persons=13 percent. This represents an average of one person per church in a one-month period.

Churches One, Five and Nineteen which have two kinds of groups respectively have a total of 16.5 members in a one month period = 5.5 members each; whereas the three churches shown above have all kinds of groups, but could only attract one person each in a one month period. What this shows is that it is not really the number of small groups which a church has that matters, but it is the structure of such groups and their effectiveness in attracting and retaining members that is important.

It is evident that these churches are not operating the kind of structure that could generate exponential growth expected of churches with well-structured, intentional and attractive small groups. This is what makes the difference in the level of growth these churches experience and how spiritually engaged their members are. Thus, it is not a question of how well these churches are operating their current system, rather, it is a question of having a complete integration of a new system. George Barna, while advising on the issue writes, "Doing more of what you're doing will not take you to the next level; doing more of the same and doing it better won't get you there either. You will need to integrate new strategies and new tactics to climb to a higher plane of ministry impact and lifestyle purity."[10]

Comments

Barna predicted in one of his research findings that the traditional church structures are only likely to appeal to 35 percent of the overall population.[11] This research's outcome however, attest to the same conclusion, but with a lower rate of 28 percent, which the churches are able to appeal to with their present structure. In the chapter following, the question of feature of a healthy church with disciples that are producing other disciples will be discussed.

Chapter 6

Discipleship and Church's Health

There is a very close connection between church health and its disciple-making strategy. George Barna identifies the connectivity when he writes, "Discipleship matter because it is necessary for the church to become healthy and productive. We cannot reach our potential without spiritual growth."[1] Just as it is expedient for disciples to be equipped to maturity, so it is for the church to be totally committed to the process and strategy of equipping the disciples. It is not enough for the church to emphasize quantitative growth at the expense of spiritual growth, which determines the quality of the members. Barna, in the same report says, "Growing true disciples is a major undertaking of the church."[7] This has been the missing link in most of the churches, and it is precisely what this book is set out to highlight for the attention of church leaders.

Paul, in his writings, figuratively describes the church as the Body of Christ. For example, he says to the church in Ephesus, "And hath put all things under his feet, and gave him to be the head overall things to the *church,* which is his *body*, the fullness of him that filled all in all" (Eph 1:22-23, emphasis added). Jesus is the Head of the church, and the church is His body.

In the same epistle, Paul uses another analogy to describe the relationship between Jesus and the church. Invoking the familiar language of family sociology, Paul likened the dynamic connection between the Church and Christ to the relationship between a husband and his wife. He writes, "For the husband is the head of the wife, even as Christ is the head of the church, and he is the savior of the body" (Eph 5:23).

Since the Head (Christ) is described as "the savior of the body," there is no doubt that the Head is perfect, and is performing its functions of directing the body adequately. However, it is necessary to determine the condition of the body. This is where the problem is, because presently, the church of Christ seems not to be in its best condition. Let us take a closer look at the operation of the church by considering the performance of the body constituents.

Examining the Various Parts of the Body/Church

In the three Scriptural references where Paul wrote about the various gifts in the church, he likens the operation of spiritual gifts in the church to the operation of the different parts of the human body. For instance, in describing the ministry gifts, he states,

And he gave some, apostles; and some, prophets; and some, evangelists; and some pastors and teachers. for the perfecting of the saints, for the work of the ministry for the edifying of the body of Christ. Till we all come in the unity of the faith, and of the knowledge of the Son of God, unto a perfect man, unto the measure of the stature of the fullness of Christ . . . From whom the whole body fitly joined together and compacted by that which every joint supplieth, according to the effectual working in the measure of every part, maketh increase of the body unto the edifying of itself in love (Eph 4: 11-16).

This passage describes the basic responsibility of church leaders commonly referred to as "the five-fold ministry" in developing believers into spiritual maturity. Since there is no categorization or qualification of the *saints*, it means that all the believers under the leadership of the church are to be *perfected* the "work of the ministry, and for the edification of the body of Christ." The *saints* represent the individual parts of the body which are "fitted and held together by what every joint supply." Thus, it is the effectiveness and health of each part that makes the growth and health of the body possible. This means that the body cannot grow beyond the well being of the individual part that makes up the body. Therefore, for the body to be healthy, attention must be given to the health of the individual members that makes up the body. Similarly, the growth of the church is dependent on the growth of the individual members. As the members are equipped and developed into maturity, so also would the church grow in quality and quantity.

However, there is a divergence in what the church is doing and what this Scriptures prescribes. While the church tries to grow some members of the congregation to maturity at the expense of the larger part, the church must adopt a strategy whereby all the members would be trained and equipped together for the work of ministry.

Paul emphasized the same point when he writes in another passage, "When we preach, warning every man, and teaching every man in all wisdom; that we may present every man perfect in Christ Jesus (Col 1:28). In this passage, Paul's preaching and teaching was to *every man,* with the sole aim of making them perfect in Christ. Therefore, the strategy of church growth should be growing everyone in the church in order to make every member perfect in Christ.

In another Paul's writing on the "gifts of the Spirit," Paul says,

> *But now are they many members, yet but one body . . . Nay, much more those members   of the body, which seem to be more feeble, are necessary; For our comely parts have no need; but God hath tempered the body together, having*

*given more abundant honor to that part which
lacked; that there should be no schism in the
body; but that the members should have the same
body; but that the members should have the same
care one for another (1Cor 12:20-25)*

The message in this text is that though each members of
the body performs different functions, with some
members occupying some more prominent positions than
the others, yet, all the parts should be treated equally and
with dignity because all of them function to complement
one another and for the overall interest of the body.

The question then is this: How is this analogy
related and applicable to the church? The common
arrangement in the church today is to encourage a part of
the congregation to be involved in the church ministries,
leaving a larger part undeveloped, reducing them to
spectators. This is contrary to Paul's recommendation of
the connectivity of the parts. "Whether one member
suffers, all the members suffer with it..." This is why the
church suffers as some of the members are made
redundant by not being developed, whereas as Allen
Hadidian has observed, "Discipling strengthens the
church body, and perpetuates God's work by developing
godly leaders for the church."[3]

Features of a Disciple-Making Church

From the above observation, the picture of a disciple-making church is getting clearer, and so in this section, I intend to identify some features that are common to such churches, using the early church as the benchmark. About the early church, the Bible says,

> *And they continued steadfast in the apostles'*
> *doctrine and fellowship, and in the breaking of*
> *bread, and in prayer. And fear came upon every*
> *soul; and many wonders and signs were done by*
> *the apostles. And all that believed were*
> *together, and had all things in common; And*
> *sold their possessions and goods, and*
> *parted them to all men as every man had need.*
> *And they continuing daily with one accord in*
> *the temple, and breaking bread from house to*
> *house did eat their meat with gladness and*
> *singleness of heart. Praising God, and*
> *having favor with the people. and the Lord added*
> *to the church daily such as be saved (Acts 2: 42-*
> *47).*

There are ten different habits that set the early church apart. These are: studying the Apostles' teaching, fellowshipping with each other, breaking bread together, prayer, unity, meeting needs, meeting in the temple, breaking bread from house to house, praising God, and having favor with all the people.

In the operation of the early church, they were bonded together as a community. They were together expressing their love and affection to one another in the best way possible. There is no doubt that their operation was immersed in an environment of mutual relationship and community. This is most likely the reason why God kept "adding to the church daily such as should be saved." Individual growth usually leads to corporate growth. As seen in the example of the early church, there are three identifiable characteristics of a healthy church. First, they are deliberate and fervent in their disciple-making efforts. It is not a process they stumble upon, but a strategy they deliberately adopt.

Second, their approach is individual centered. Every member is considered as an important and integral part of the church, which makes the overall growth of the church possible. There is every reason to believe that the church will grow steadily as they intentionally develop and nurture every individual to attain their full potential.

Third, the motive of the church is missional, which is the divine task that the church has been mandated to carry out—to go and make disciples of all nations. As already pointed out in Chapter four, members grow better in small group structure where they are able to develop and nurture their gifts effectively.

How Healthy is the Body of Christ?

The research findings show that the church as a whole is not in its best state of health, with individual churches showing different conditions of ill health. Apart from structures and programs of the church which have been discussed in the research findings, another noticeable factor that could be responsible for the church's conditions is the spiritual food the congregations are being fed with by those who have the oversight over them. Just as the food a person is fed with determines his/her well being in the natural, so also it is in the spiritual. The spiritual well being of the congregation is determined by the spiritual food they are being fed with. In what follows, I will borrow from nutritional metaphor and imageries to describe the spiritual state of the churches today.

Seven Kinds of Bodies/Churches: A Metaphor of Anatomy and Physiology

1. **Hemiplegic Body/Church**. This is the kind of church which engages half of its congregation in small group activities including ushering, choir, welcoming guests, women's fellowship, men's fellowship, youth ministry, children's ministry, etc., but leaves the other half as spectators. Although, this other half is counted as members, they are not productive members. This typifies

a body that is half paralyzed, and half active, which would make the church need some serious therapy to activate the paralyzed half, and the whole body.

2. Emaciated Body/Church. This is the kind of church that shows serious nutrition deficiency. It is a church that has no development program, and all that the leadership provides for the congregation could be compared to a cold meal served only on Sunday morning. The church remains underfed, and has no form of nutrition for a whole week. This typical church is weightless, making members unable to perform any form of spiritual responsibility, including soul winning.

3. Shunted Body/Church. This is the kind of church that is fed with the food meant for another kind of body. When fed with wrong diet, the body is shunted instead of growing properly. This typifies those churches whose leaders feed their congregations with copied sermons, and internet generated messages, instead of serving them with relevant messages that would inspire and give them the proper inspiration and motivation towards their situations. Instead of proper growth the church is spiritually shunted.

4. Cancerous Body/Church. The cancer may be benign or malignant. In either case, a body with an early stage of cancer might look physically healthy, but on proper diagnosis, a particular kind of cancer at some stage of growth could be detected. This is the kind of church that looks good on the outside due to its sheer size or structure, but is completely disoriented by internal strives and conflicts which makes the development of their members difficult. The fact that the people are not bonded together by the essential elements of love, the Holy Spirit finds it difficult to operate freely, and the people end up splitting into different fragments, which would eventually leads to the demise of the church.

5. Exhausted Body/Church. There are some people who misuse their bodies, and because they do not understand the body's warning signs, the body breaks down due to exhaustion. This is the kind of church that is busy with mostly irrelevant programs and activities round the year. For the fact that they are just doing programs that may or may not relate to their vision, and the people's spiritual needs, the people are soon burnt out. Such programs also do not add to the church both numerically and spiritually. Because the people do not gain any benefit from the programs, and because they are exhausted, they react by gradually keeping away from the programs, until they stop going to church altogether.

6. Anemic Body/Church. Anemia is a medical condition where blood is not enough to keep the body and the essential vital organs running effectively. If care is not taken, it could lead to death. The blood goes through the arteries and nourishes the entire body. By not providing effective tools for discipling, what the churches are doing is to deny their members (the arteries of their congregations) the essential spiritual blood needed for daily living.

7. Kwashiorkored Body/Church. Kwashiorkor is a disease of extreme malnourishments. It occurs quite often in the time of war when food is in short supplies and people, especially children, have to feed on food lacking in proteins and essential nutrition. The stomach is always swollen and the body is weak. There are some churches that are experiencing this kind of ailment in the spiritual. They are overfed but undernourished. They are barraged on all sides by ideologies, doctrines, rules of dos and don'ts, and philosophies that are completely of no spiritual relevance; and so, the churches are sick almost to the point of death.

Although, some churches have been identified in their different stages of inactivity or derelictions, the good news is that such churches could still become healthy and vibrant. Since the ability to be fruitful is in every living thing, all it takes for the seed to be fruitful is to be in the right environment and have the necessary conditions, which the next chapter will consider as it relates to the church.

CHAPTER 7

The Church and Fruitfulness of Believers

Shortly before Jesus gave the church its assignment to go and make disciples of all nations, He declared, "All power is given unto me in heaven and in earth" (Matt 28:19). By this affirmation, Jesus wanted to let the church know that the assignment is to be carried out on the basis of His power and authority which had been given to Him over the whole universe. Also, Jesus wanted to make the disciples know that the scope of their assignment was the whole universe. Thus, the church must see itself as the vehicle of Christ's mission to the world, and such a vehicle must not just be functional, but must be operational at the highest level of performance.

God created every living thing with the potential to reproduce itself, which implies fruitfulness. This inherent ability to be fruitful is traceable to God's blessing on His creation. For instance, when God created the living things in the waters and in the air, He blessed them, "Be fruitful, and multiply, and fill the waters in the seas, and let fowl multiply in the earth" (Gen 1:22). So, also did God bless man, "Be fruitful, and multiply, and replenish the earth, and subdue it: and have dominion over the fish of the sea, and over the fowl of the air, and over every living thing that moveth upon the earth" (Gen 1:28).

So, also is the church, which is described as God's *special possession*. The Bible says, "But you are a chosen people, a royal priesthood, a holy nation, God's special possession..." (2 Pet 2:9, NAS). As God's special possession, the church is supposed to be vibrant and possess the ability to be fruitful by reproducing itself like other living things many times over. Thus, the church must have the ability and potential to cover the earth as it disciples all nations. One could see the similarity between the church's assignment and the *assignment* of every living thing to reproduce itself until it replenishes and subdues the earth.

Since the research outcome has pointed to the fact that the church is not doing enough to justify its ability to reproduce and multiply itself as it makes disciples (see Chapter 5), it is necessary to offer some suggestions for the church's fruitfulness so that the church could break off from its characteristic unfruitfulness, and begin on the path of fruitfulness.

What is Fruitfulness?

What is fruitfulness? Simply stated, it is the ability to bear fruit. Michael Adebiyi writing on the subject of fruitfulness, defines fruitfulness as "The process of one's potential to produce viable output, a healthy growth, the ability to bear fruit in abundance, to be prolific, or productive."[1] Therefore, for any living thing to dominate its environment, it must have the potential to bear fruit for the purpose of reproducing itself. It is when it bears fruit that it can multiply through its seed. Reflecting on the effect of fruitfulness on globalization, Adebiyi writes, "The day you begin to apply the system, making global impact begins.[2]"

In the biblical context, fruitfulness could also mean *good works* The Bible says, "For we are his workmanship, created in Christ Jesus unto good works, which God hath before ordained that we walk in them" (Eph 2:10). Thus, every believer is created for the purpose of performing good works that God has designed for them well before they were born. It is the same thing God told Jeremiah, "Before I formed thee in the belly I knew thee; and before thou camest forth out of the womb I sanctified thee, and I ordained thee a prophet unto the nations (Jere 1:5). Therefore, the *good works* which everyone has been created to perform here on earth is the purpose for which they have been created. This is why every person's purpose is different from the other person's, just as no two persons are created the same. Every person is unique, and fashioned specifically for his/her assignment.

From the Metaphoric to the Empirical

In this segment, I will provide a componential analysis by looking at the dichotomy of the metaphoric and the empirical application. There is a continuum between the realm of the physical and that of the spiritual. This is why the Lord employed the pedagogy of parables, allegories, and analogies in making sense of heavenly things on earth. Fruitfulness is the crucible of the Christian faith. Jesus Christ made it such a central discourse in His parting message to them that He devoted quality time to teaching His disciples the overarching value of fruitfulness for the continuity and perpetuity of his ministry.

For example, the Lord invoked the organic metaphor of the vine, the vinedresser and the branches, where there is a responsorial relationship among the three, identifying the essence of such relationship as fruitfulness. Without fruitfulness that relationship turns sour because the vine and vinedresser would not continue to keep a branch that is unfruitful. The analogy of the vine and its branches states,

I am the true vine, and my Father is the husbandman. Every branch in me that beareth not fruit he taketh away: and every branch that beareth fruit, he purgeth it, that it may bring forth more fruit. Now ye are clean through the word which I have spoken unto you. Abide in me, and I

in you. As the branch cannot bear fruit of itself, except it abide in the vine; no more can ye, except ye abide in me. I am the vine, ye are the branches: He that abideth in me, and I in him, the same bringeth forth much fruit: for without me ye can do nothing. If a man abide not in me, he is cast forth as a branch, and is withered; and men gather them, and cast them into the fire, and they are burned. If ye abide in me, and my words abide in you, ye shall ask what ye will, and it shall be done unto you. Herein is my Father glorified, that ye bear much fruit; so shall ye be my disciples (Jn 15:1-8).

In this Scripture, God's expectation of every believer is not just to bear fruit, but to bear much fruit; and for the fruit to remain, because that is what gives God glory. Bruce Wilkinson identifies four levels of fruit bearing from this passage: no fruit, fruit, more fruit, and much fruit.[2]

Level 1: No Fruit

"Every branch in me that beareth not fruit," (v. 2). These are believers who have nothing to show as their contribution to the kingdom in terms of their good works. They make no impact whatsoever in the lives of others, and as a result, they have no reflection that could influence their environment. These are believers who are not essentially different from unbelievers as they

probably have not yet discovered their life purpose, and as a result, have no good works to show.

What is God's reaction to the branch that does not bear fruit? *He taketh away* (v. 2). What does it mean for God to *take away* the branch that is unproductive? The common understanding is that God destroys the branch as it is thrown into the fire. This notion is not correct because the phrase *take away* in Greek is *(airo)*, which simply means, *lift up*. It is the same root word with the phrase *take away* when Jesus told the paralytic man to *take up* his bed (Matt 9:6). Thus, *take away* does not mean to *cut off* or *burn up* or *die*. The Greek word, *(airo)* means *to lift up* and *take away* from the ground to tie on a trellis. The Vinedresser's intention is not to destroy the branch, but to make it productive. When the believer continues to be unfruitful, God reacts by chastening (a sort of rebuke) him/her.

> *"And you have forgotten the exhortation which speaks to you as to sons: My son, do not despise the chastening of the Lord, nor be discouraged when you are rebuked by Him; for whom the Lord loves He chastens, and scourges every son whom he receives" (Heb 12:5).*

God chastens every believer at one time or the other in his/her life. Thus, God's chastening is a universal experience for all born-again believers. God's intention for chastening is to nurture and stimulate fruitfulness. It is very likely that some of the congregations that have been identified in the survey as not doing enough to justify their fruitfulness are likely to be undergoing God's chastening process. It is hoped that when you are going through this process you would understand and appreciate what God is doing in your life as His intention is to make you fruitful, no matter how painful the experience could be.

Level 2: Fruit

"And every branch that beareth fruit" (v. 2). These are Christians who are producing some fruit of good works in their Christian lives. As already identified in the operation of small groups, Christians have the great opportunity of caring for one another, and assisting members to perform good works in their Christian walk. This is what fruitfulness entails. However, God is not satisfied with barely enough or *some fruit,* but wants everyone to operate at his/her optimal level of fruitfulness. What does God do to get these people to become more fruitful?

In the context of the passage, what does the Vinedresser's reaction to branches that produce some fruit? "And every branch that beareth fruit, he purgeth (prunes, NIV) it, that it may bring forth more" (v. 2). *Pruning* reveals God's primary goal for every branch that bears some fruit so that it may bear more fruit. Thus, pruning is the primary method that the Vinedresser applies to make branches more productive. This means that as the believer begins to bear fruit, the process of pruning begins, so that he/she may bear more fruit. Pruning is the process of helping you reallocate your primary resources for greater potential because the only way you can get more is by doing less of the unprofitable things. It is possible that it was after Paul had gone through the process of pruning that he learned to concentrate in doing one thing. He wrote, "This one thing I do..." (Phil 3:14).

There are certain things that need to be redirected in your life for greater productivity. These include the use of your time, talent, money, life purpose, and your heart passion to serve others. Pruning could take place at numerous times during the season, and could involve the use of different tools in order to prune most effectively. It is after the pruning that the fruit sprouts, and not during the process. So it is for a believer.

You may ask, "How do I know that I am going through pruning?" The answer is simple. When you think more about the meaning of life, or what God wants you to do. It could happen as you determine to serve God, or as you release past failures to focus on the future. In the final analysis, pruning lessens the pleasure you experience from unfruitful activities.

Level 3: More Fruit

"And every branch that beareth fruit, he purges that it may bring forth more fruit" (v. 2). This is the level at which believers begin to bear more fruit as they are

pruned. They are able to concentrate more on what God has called them to do, and less on the unprofitable things. They are more responsible and accountable. While at this level, believers are able to make their impact felt in the lives of other people as they demonstrate God's love to neighbors and fellow believers. They are able to do more of good works as true disciple of Christ, basically because they have discovered their life purpose, and have set themselves to fulfilling it. Yet, God has not finished with them, for He would want them to produce much fruit.

What is God's expectation of you as you begin to operate at this level? "He that abideth in me, and I in him, the same bringeth forth much fruit" (v. 5). God wants you to bear much fruit because that is His ultimate expectation of every believer. Thus, He would want you to keep *abiding* in Him.

What does it mean to abide? "abide" means to continue to be present, and not to depart. The same meaning is as reflected in the context of this passage, "But they constrained him, saying, Abide with us: for it is toward evening, and the day is far spent. And he went in to tarry with them" (Lk 24:29). *Abiding* in the vineyard occurs at the place where the branch and the vine are joined together, which is not easily detachable. This is the kind of relationship that should exist between someone at this level and God. This is why much fruit is produced here and why Jesus said "Without me ye can do nothing" (v. 5). In the vineyard, the branch produces much fruit in quantity of the clusters, size of the fruit, and in its quality.

There are two kinds of *abiding* specified in the Scriptures. First, is the *abiding* that takes place at salvation. At salvation, the believer is said to be *in Christ*. This is done for the believer by God, and he/she receives it as a gift. Second, is the *fruit bearing abiding*. This kind of abiding cannot be done by God, but by the believer as he/she is obedient to God, and has regular fellowship and deep intimacy with Him. For clarification, it could be said that all believers *abide in Christ*, but few *abide with Christ*. Until a believer gets to this level of abiding with Christ, it is not possible to produce much fruit. Many believers try to bear fruit by hard work without abiding, only to end up achieving very little or nothing.

Level 4: Much Fruit

"I am the vine, ye are the branches; He that abideth in me, and I in him, the same bringeth forth much fruit; for without me ye can do nothing" (v. 5). At the level of *much fruit*, you become a *light* in your world that cannot be hidden. You are able to reproduce yourself many times over in others, as an evidence of your fruitfulness. At this level, you would be able to do as Paul admonished Timothy, "And the things that thou hast heard of me among many witnesses, the same commit thou to faithful men, who shall be able to teach others also" (2 Tim 2:2). Production of much fruit is both in the quantity and quality of the fruit.

What is do You Think God is Doing in Your Life now?

What God is doing in your life right now is determined by your level of fruitfulness, which in turn, is determined by your church's level of fruitfulness. This is quite revealing in the research findings in Chapter five for the 20 churches surveyed. The rate at which they were able to attract and retain their first time guests, when taken as the member's "good works," was determined at 28 percent. This means that the church as a whole is producing at the rate of 28 percent. The is the level of *fruit*.

When each of the 20 churches is considered along with the rate at which it is able to attract and retain its first time guests, the breakdown is as follows:

- 12 churches representing 60% of the churches produce less than 2 new converts in a one month period = no fruit
- 5 churches which represents 25% of the churches produce less than 5 new converts in a one month period = some fruit.
- 2 churches which represents 10% of the churches produce less than 10 new converts in a one month period = more fruit
- 1 church which represents 5% of the churches produce 40 plus new converts in a one month

period = much fruit

See how these levels are depicted in table 1.1 below.

Level of fruit Bearing	No of churches	Quantity of Fruit	% of Churches
Level 1	12	No Fruit	60%
Level 2	5	Some Fruit	25%
Level 3	2	More Fruit	10%
Level 4	1	Much Fruit	5%

Table 1.1., Showing percentage of churches in each level of fruit bearing

When the church is taken as an assembly of believers, every believer could identify his/her level of fruitfulness in line with their church's fruitfulness. From the above table, it shows that 60 percent of believers are without any fruit, while 25 percent are producing some fruit, and 10 percent are producing more fruit, only 5 percent produce much fruit.

As already stated, your level of fruitfulness will determine what God is doing in your life. If you are at the level of *no fruit*, I hope you are listening to God's chastening, as He *takes you up* to be able to produce some fruit. For those who are presently producing some fruit, there is no doubt that God wants you to produce more as He *prunes* you. For those at the level of *more fruit*, God is presently asking you to *abide* so that you could produce much fruit.

Table 1.2 below clarifies what God is doing in believers' lives at their level of fruitfulness.

No fruit to Some Fruit	Fruit to More Fruit	More fruit to Much Fruit
What is God doing in your life as you are not bearing fruit?	What is God doing in your life as you bear fruit, and He wants you to bear more fruit?	What does God desire you to do in order to grow from bearing more to much fruit?
He "taketh away"	He "prunes"	You "abide"

Table 1.2., Showing God's reaction in each level of fruit bearing

What Should the Church Do to Take Believers to Optimal Level?

And he gave some, apostles; and some, prophets; and some, evangelists; and some, pastors and teachers; For the perfecting of the saints, for the work of the ministry, for the edifying of the body of Christ: Till we all come in the unity of the faith, and of the knowledge of the Son of God, unto a perfect man, unto the measure of the stature of the fullness of Christ.

This Scripture shows that the church also has some role to play in the lives of believers through church leaders. Church leaders, usually referred to as "The fivefold ministry," are given to the church "for the perfecting" of believers for the work of ministry, and for the edification of the body of Christ. "Perfecting" means "equipping," or "empowering." This process involves the conscious efforts of the leaders to develop believers so that they could be full of good works as they make their impact felt in their communities.

This is to say that the development and fruitfulness of every believer is to be fashioned through some process of growth. Michael Adebiyi refers to this process as "system of fruitfulness,"[2] which he said is in three stages. These are the stages of discovery, development, and deployment.

System of Fruitfulness

Stage one: Discovery

Discovery, in the agriculture context, is the process of discovering the seed, the land, and the weeds. This implies that every seed is made to produce on a particular kind of soil. Thus, it is for the farmer to identify his seed, and determine the kind of land that is most suitable for the seed. Then, the farmer is to ensure that the growth and productivity of the seed is taken care of. What is the implication of this principle to the church?

As established earlier, every believer is endowed with the seed of greatness that is referred to variously as talent, gifts, calling, and ability. The Bible confirms, *"The Holy Spirit... dividing to everyone severally as he will" (1 Cor 12:11).* This implies that every believer, irrespective of their background or physical make up, has got a kind of gift, skill or ability for good works, which the church leaders are expected to help them to discover.

However, the present system of the church by which members are kept on the pews as spectators without involving them productively in discipling activities has not been helping them to develop their gifts. Some of them do not even know if they have any gift at all, making such gifts unutilized and, unproductive.

For the seed to produce, it needs the right kind of soil. Similarly, the right kind of environment for the members to discover their gifts and skills, as earlier stipulated, is the environment of small groups. This is the place where the leadership, administrative, healing, evangelism, and other gifts could be discovered and helped to flourish. In small groups, each one has an opportunity to be used by God to minister to the others in the group. Thus, it is in the environment of small groups that individuals could be motivated to bring out the best in them as they are given the opportunity to exhibit their skills, unlike in the church environment where the opportunity is limited. This is why Adebiyi surmises, "If you do not create an enabling environment for your seed, it will not yield."[3]

It is also in small groups that every form of obstructions that could affect the growth of the seed could be effectively taken care of including character flaws like anger, ignorance, covetousness, and laziness.

In small groups, it is not easy for members to put up ungodly character and attitude without being picked up for corrected by other members of the group. As a matter of fact, every member would want to align with what looks like the group's code of ethics in character and conduct.

Allen Hadidian expresses the same idea in his analogy of natural parents nurturing their children to maturity. He opined that it is natural to assume that in the spiritual realm, those who are more mature are to care for those who are less mature. He deposed that many struggle with sin in the church because there is no one who is willing to show personal concern.[4] Without any doubt, the small groups provide the right environment for the moral discipline of their members, which the bigger structure of the church might find cumbersome to accomplish.

Stage Two: Development

In the plant culture, the most critical stage in its development process is nurturing the plant to fruition. It is whatever happens to the plant at this stage that determines its productivity, or lack thereof. So it is in the spiritual growth of each individuals in the church which determines the overall health of the church. As Adebiyi rightly noted, "Seeds naturally look tiny, but when sowed, they unfold great potentials.' He warns, "Don't be deceived by the size of your seed; it is not usually big."[5] A well-nurtured seed has an unlimited potential. This fact is predicated on the assumption that fruitfulness is an attribute of nature and nurture, the latter being a greater responsibility of the human effort.

Thus, every person's gift must be considered very important for the spiritual growth of the individual, and the overall growth of the church, because everyone has been given his/her gift as the Holy Spirit deems fit. Also, in a small group structure, every member has one responsibility or the other to carry out in the group, which aids the growth and development of their potentials. For instance, there are people who prepare the meeting venue, by arranging chairs and tables for the meeting. Another person could be in charge of following up with the absentees to know why they are absent, while another could be responsible for cleaning up the venue after the meeting.

As simple as these responsibilities might seem, they are to sharpen members' skills, and in the process, the seemingly dormant potential would begin to emerge, and be developed into maturity, leading to greater responsibilities. This is the key to fruitfulness, which is highly recommended for every church to adopt for the spiritual growth of their members, culminating in the spiritual growth of the church as a whole.

Stage Three: Deployment

Deployment is the final stage of development. "This is the maturing stage of your talent... and the time for launching out."[6]This stage requires hard work, and it is also a time of celebration. This is the stage in which a leader releases a qualified apprentice graduates to start his/her own group. It has been observed that this is the most exciting time in the life of a Christian--when a believer sees his/her convert lead another convert to Christ and develops the convert to his/her maturity and fruitfulness..

As the groups keep splitting and multiplying, so would the church be growing because the underlining reason for the group's togetherness is to bring more people from the community into their fold. Cho's opinion agrees with this assertion. He writes, "Groups that meet without having evangelism as a goal do not produce growth in the church."[7] It is also when groups keep splitting that new churches are planted. Cho also states, "As each cell grows and begins to divide, you'll soon have a church."[8]

This is the same principle that multinational companies use in having their influence spread to the nations of the world. Adebiyi identifies Chick-Fil-A as one of such companies, which started in 1946 as a restaurant, but which today has 975 franchises through an effective system of distribution of its fruit.[9] When the church adopts this system of fruitfulness, there is no doubt that they too would experience the kind of exponential growth as other organizations that are applying this system and are enjoying the fruit of their efforts. As expected, the church also would be in a position to disciple all nations.

CHAPTER 8

Conclusion

"For we are his workmanship, created in Christ Jesus unto good works, which God hath before ordained that we should walk in them" (Eph. 2:10). This is man's purpose on earth. We are created in Christ Jesus ever before the foundation of the earth--for the purpose of showing forth good works. As already explained, "good works" is not necessarily what we put up to be saved, as we are not saved by works, but by grace (Eph 2:8). Rather, these are deeds we put up as believers so as to reflect God's goodness to others, and for God to be glorified. Although, the good works we are expected to walk in have been created for us before we were born, it is every person's responsibility to discover them and determine to walk in them.

The essence of a successful life is discovering one's life purpose and walking in it. If you do not discover your life goal, it is very difficult to aspire to walk in what you do not know, talk less of being fruitful in it. This is where many Christians are still struggling today. They live the life of their own, which turns out to be a purposeless life. This makes them do things that are not pleasing to God. I hope that from what you have read in this book, you would seek to discover your life purpose and aspire to walk in it from the moment you discover it.

Another thing that should be clear in our mind is that whatever life you live, and whatever level of fruitfulness you find yourself in, it is what you do on earth that would determine your eternal reward. Think on this Scripture,

> *"Wherefore we labor, that, whether present or absent, we may be accepted of him. For we must all appear before the judgment seat of Christ; that every one may receive the things done in his body, according to that he hath done, whether it   be good or bad" (2 Cor 5:9-10).*

Thus, when you stand before the judgment seat of Christ, what reward are you expecting? There is no doubt that we would be rewarded according to our good works here on earth. The Parable of the Talent attests to this fact (Matt 25:14-30).

In the parable, God reacted differently to the three servants. For the two servants that double their talents, the Master commended them as "good and faithful servants" (Matt 25: 21, 23), However, for the servant who, for whatever reason buried his talent under the earth, the Master described him as "wicked and slothful"

(v. 26), and was ordered to be cast into the "outer darkness: there will be weeping and gnashing of teeth" (v. 30).

It is possible to know the mind of God from the treatment given to these servants. God wants everyone to be profitable and fruitful as we utilize whatever talent or resources that are available for our use for the promotion of God's kingdom. This is why the master commanded that the talent of the unprofitable servant should be given to the one who had ten talents, because *"unto every one that hath shall be given, and he shall have abundance: but from him that hath not shall be taken away even that which he hath"* (v. 29).

I want to admonish you that at every step of your Christian walk, you must be responsive to God's reaction because His intention is not to *cast you away* but to make you more productive. When He prunes you, you must know that He wants to make you concentrate on those areas of your strength and calling so that you would bring forth more fruit. If you are already bringing forth more fruit, He wants you to *abide*, and be in perfect intimacy with Him, so that you would be able to bring forth much fruit.

Every church leader must take their calling seriously because you will give account of every soul that God gives you to nurture. Are you nurturing them for their fruitfulness, or you are using them to build your church? What contributions are you making in their lives? Listen to Paul's admonition to Titus, "And let ours also learn to maintain good works for necessary uses, that they be not unfruitful."

As you read these words, I pray that the lessons may resonate with you and meet you at every point of your Christian faith so that you may be a partaker of God's commendation for the good and faithful servant.

You should also note that the recommendation of fruitfulness, which this book has emphasized, is not a sort of happenstance approach, but a principle that must be consciously worked out for the best interest of the believers in particular, and the church as a whole because it lines up with the way God has set up every living thing to multiply and perpetuate itself on earth.

I want to suggest that while churches' leaders begin to apply the principles of fruitfulness, they should look into the methods that suit their culture and environment. For instance, there are some places where people would not want to come to church no matter the inducement. However, when they are invited to homes, or you take the gospel to them at the point of their needs, it is very likely that they would be responsive. With proper presentation of the gospel, they could be led to Christ and eventually to the church.

There are some churches that already have small groups, but are not producing fruit, I recommend that such groups should be slowly disbanded, and be replaced with productive ones as described in this book, or as the Holy Spirit might minister to you. There is no doubt that this process requires the personal commitment of the church leader. This is because if the pastor is not involved, any groups set up cannot be effective. Cho states, "Without the pastor, the system will not hold together"[1] Also, groups must be conscious that they are together for one purpose only—for evangelism. It has been proved that "groups that meet without having evangelism as a goal do not produce growth in the church."[2]

The church leaders have the responsibility of communicating the process and activities of the small groups to the members of the church, so that members could resonate with it as it develops to become the church's culture, especially with the emphasis that every member should belong to one group or the other. Educating members about group formation and its advantages must be an ongoing process through the church's newsletter, notice board, church bulletin, and other announcement opportunities.

When church leaders take these suggestions into consideration, there is no doubt that they would begin to experience the kind of growth and relevance expected of their churches, as the community begins to feel their impact. Also, members would be able to show their spiritual maturity in their words and deeds. This is what the church is designed for and what would make it to fulfill its task of discipling the nations of the world.

NOTES

Introduction

1. Terry Bowland, *Make Disciples* (Joplin, MO: College Press Publications, 1999), 18.

2. Aubrey Malphurs, *A New Kind of Church: Understanding Models of Ministry for the 21st Century* (Grand Rapids, MI: Baker Books, 2007), 75.

3. Ibid., 17-18..

4. Ibid., 12.

5. George Barna, *Growing True Disciples* (Colorado Springs: Water brook Press, 2001), 11.

Chapter 1: Biblical and Pastoral Theologies

1. Jeffrey Arnold, *Starting Small Groups: Building Communities that Matter* (Nashville, TN: Abingdon Press, 1997), 23.

2. Ibid., 21.

3. David Yonggi Cho, *Successful Home Cell Groups* (Gainesville, FL: Bridge-Logos Publishers 1981), 49.

4. Oswald Sanders, *Spiritual Discipleship: Principles of following Christ for Every Believer* (Chicago, IL: Moody Publishers, 1990), 8.

5. George Barna, 18.

6. Ibid., 24.

7. Barna, *The Power of Vision* (Ventura, CA: Regal, 1992), 24.

8. Barna, *Disciples,* 130.

9. Ibid.

10. Ibid.

11. Ibid.

12. Andy Stanley and Bill Willits, *Creating Community: 5 Keys to Building a Small Group Culture* (Sisters, OR: Multnomah Publishers, 2004), 95.

13..Barna, 127.

Chapter 2: Discipleship

1.. Gordon Ferguson, *The Victory of Surrender* (Billerica, MS: Discipleship Publications International, 2003), 56.

2. George Barna, *Growing True Disciples* (Colorado Springs: Water brook Press, 2001), 24.

3 Barna, Disciples, 30.

4. Ibid., 10.

5. Ferguson, Victory, 29

Chapter 3: Leadership

1. Jim Collins, *Good to Great* (New York, NY: Haper Collins Publishers Inc.), 28.

2. Ibid., 21.

3. Ibid., 41.

4 Ibid.

5. Ibid., 13.

6. Ibid., 42

7. Ibid., 13

8. John C. Maxwell, *Developing the Leader within You* (Nashville, TN: Thomas Nelson, Inc.), 2.

9. Kouzes and Posner, *The Christian Reflection on Leadership Challenge* (San Francisco, CA: John Wiley & Sons, Inc.), 2.

10. Ibid., 2.

11. Maxwell, 5.

12. Paul W. Powell, *Getting the Lead out of Leadership* (Tyler, TX), 55.

13. Kouzes and Posner, 120.

14. Ibid.

15. Maxwell, 39.

16. Collins, 17.

17. Kouzes and Posner, 72.

18. Maxwell, 75.

19. Powell, 108.

20. Kouzes and Posner,

21. Ibid., 128.

Chapter 4: Leadership Development Structure

1. Dave Earley, *Turning Members into Leaders* (Houston, TX: Cell Group Resources), 33.

2. Ibid., 37

3. Jeffrey Arnold, *Starting Small Groups: Building Communities that Matter* (Nashville, TN: Abingdon Press), 11.

4. Ibid., 17.

5. Ibid., 17.

6. Ibid., 17.

7. Ibid., 18.

8. Leith Anderson, *A Church for the 21st Century* (Minneapolis, MN: Bethany House Publishers), 36.

9. David Yonggi Cho, *Successful Home Cell Groups* (Gainesville, FL: bridge-Logos Publishers), 63.

10. Neal F. McBride, *How to Lead Small Groups* (Colorado springs, CO: NavPress, 1990), 19.

11. Ibid., 17.

12. Yonggi Cho, 70.

13. Joel Comiskey, *The Church that Multiplies: Growing a Healthy Cell Church in North America* (Moreno Valley, CA: CCS Publishing, 2002), 55-59.

14. Ibid., 55.

15. Ibid., 56.

16. Ibid., 57.

17. Ibid., 59.

18. Ibid.

19. Ibid., 58.

20. Ibid.

21. Ibid., 58.

22 .Ibid.

23. Ibid., 59.

24. Ibid.

25. Ibid.

26. Ibid., 60.

27. Stephen D. Renn ed., *Expository Dictionary of Bible Words* (Peabody, MS: Hendrickson Publishers Inc., 2005).

28. Cho, 47.

29. Ibid., 48.

30. Ibid., 49.

31. Stanley and Willits, 96.

32. Cho, 51-64.

33. For the full list of the fifty-nine "one another" in the New Testament, see Carl George's *Prepare to Grow Your Church for the Future* (Tarrytown, NY: Fleming H Revel Company 1991), 129 – 131.

Chapter 5: The Church's Empirical Growth Pattern

1. Stephens D. Renn, *Expository Dictionary of Bible Words* (Peabody, MS: Hendrickson Publishers, 2005).

2. Elmer Towns and Ed Stetzer, *Perimeters of Light* (Chicago, IL: Moody Publishers, 2004), 66.

3. Dale Earley, *Turning Members into Leaders* (Houston, TX: Cell Group Resources, 2004), 17.

4. David Yonggi Cho, *Successful Home Cell Groups* (Carnesville, FL: Bridge-Logs Publications, 1981), 168.

5. Ibid., 77.

6. Slaughter, 89.

7. Earley, 88.

8. Henry Clouds and John Townsend, *Making Small Groups Work* (Grand Rapids, MI: Zondervan, 2000), 14.

9. Joel Comiskey, *The Church that Multiplies: Growing a Healthy Cell Church in North America* (Moreno Valley, CA: CCS Publishing, 2007), 50.

10. George Barna, *Growing True Disciples* (Colorado Springs, CO: Water brook Press, 2001), 10.

11. Ibid., 120.

Chapter 6: Discipleship and Church's Health.

1. Barna, Disciple, 30.

2. Ibid., 10

3. Allen Hadidian, *Successful Discipling* (Chicago, IL: Moody Press, 1979), 16.

Chapter 7: The Church and Fruitfulness of Believers

1. Michael Adebiyi, *Fruitfulness: Processing Your Potential* (Stone Mountain, GA: Principled Press Inc., 2012), 3.

2. Bruce Wilkinson, Lecture Handout titled, "What on Earth is God Doing in My Life?"

3. Adebiyi, 37.

4. Ibid., 48.

5. Hadidian, 10

6. Adebiyi, 50.

7. Ibid.

8. Ibid., 52

9. Cho, 113.

10. Ibid., 77.

11. Adebiyi, 55.

Chapter 8: Conclusion

1. Yonggi Cho, 103

2. Ibid., 113.

BIBLIOGRAPHY

Adebiyi, Michael. *Fruitfulness: Processing Your Potential*. Stone Mountain, GA: Principled press Inc., 2012.

Anderson, Leith. *A Church for the 21st Century*. Minneapolis, MN: Bethany House Publishers.

Arnold, Jeffrey. *Starting Small Groups: Building Communities that Matter*. Nashville, TN: Abingdon Press, 1997.

Barna George. *The Power of Vision*. Ventura, CA: Regal, 1992.

_____, *Growing True Disciples*. Colorado Springs, CO: Waterbrook Press 2001.

Bowland, Terry. *Make Disciples*. Joplin, MO: College Press Publications, 1999.

Cho, David Yonggi. *Successful Home Cell Groups*. Gainesville, FL: Bridge, 1981.

Clouds, Henry and John Townsend. *Making Small Groups Work*. Grand Rapids, MI: Zondervan, 2000.

Cole, Neil. *Organic Leadership*. Grand Rapids, MI. Baker Books. 2009.

Coleman, Robert E. *The Master Plan of Discipleship*. Grand Rapids, MI: Baker Books, 1998.

Collins, Jim. *Good to Great*. New York, NY: Harper Collins Publishers Inc., 2001.

Comiskey, Joel. "Cell-Based Ministry: A Positive Factor for Church Growth in Latin America." PhD diss., Fuller Theological Seminary, 1997.

_____. *Groups of 12: A New Way to Mobilize Leaders and Multiply Groups in Your Church*. Houston, TX: Touch Publications, 1999.

_____. How to be a Great Cell Group Coach. Houston, TX: TOUCH Publications, 2003.

_____. *The Church that Multiplies*. Moreno Valley, CA: CCS Publishing, 2005.

_____. *The Relational Disciple*. Moreno Valley, CA: CCS Publishing, 2010.

_____. *The Church that Multiplies: Growing a Healthy Cell Church in North America*. Moreno Valley, CA: CCS Publishing, 2007.

Cosgrove Jr. Francis. *Essentials of Discipleship*. Colorado Springs, CO: NavPress, 2009.

Dempsey. Rodney. "A Strategy to Transition a Traditional Church Educational System to a Small Group System" (D. Min. Thesis, Liberty Theological Seminary, 2004.

_____. "The Art of Developing Leaders." Lecture, CLED 974, Liberty Baptist Theological Seminary, Lynchburg, VA, January 8-12, 2012.

Donahue, Bill. *Leading Life-Changing Small Groups*. Grand Rapids, MI: Zondervan, 2002.

_____. *The Seven Deadly Sins of Small Group Ministry*. Grand Rapids, MI: Zondervan, 2002.

Driscoll, Mark. *A Book you'll actually Read: On Church Leadership*. Wheaton, IL: Crossway Books, 2008.

Earley, Dale. *Turning Members into Leaders*. Houston, TX: Cell Group Resources, 2004.

Earley, Dave, and Rod Dempsey. *The Pocket Guide to Leading a Small Group*. Houston, TX: TOUCH Publications, Inc., 2007.

Earley, Dave, and Ben Gutierrez. *Ministry is....How to Serve Jesus with Passion and Confidence.* Nashville, TN: B&H Publishing, 2010.

Egli, Jim and Dwight Marable. *Small Groups Big Impact: Connecting People to God and One Another in Thriving Groups.* Saint Charles, IL: ChurchSmart Resources, 2011.

Eims, Leroy. *The Lost Art of Disciple Making.* Grand Rapids, MI: Zondervan, 1978.

Ferguson, Gordon. *The Victory of Surrender.* Billerica, MS: Discipleship Publications International, 2003.

George, F. Carl. *Nine Keys to Effective Small Group Leadership.* Mansfield, PA. Kingdom Publishing. 1997

Hadidian, Allen. *Successful Discipling.* Chicago, IL: Moody Press, 1979.

Hestenes, Roberta. "Can Spiritual Maturity be taught?" *Leadership Journal* 4 (Fall 1988): 12-30.

Howard, David. *The Great Commission for Today.* Downers Grove, IL: Intervarsity Press, 1976.

Keating, Charles J. "Leadership and Structure."*The Catholic World*, 236 (May, 1993): 129-131.

Kouzes and Posner. *The Christian Reflection on Leadership Challenge.* San Francisco, CA: John Wiley & Sons, Inc., 2006.

Kreider, Larry. *What Every Small Group Leader Should Know.* Ventura, CA: Regal Books, 2010.

Lawless, Chuck. *Discipled Warriors: Growing Healthy Churches Equipped for Spiritual Warfare.* Grand Rapids, MI: Regal Publications, 2002.

McBride, Neal F. *How to Lead Small Groups.* Colorado Springs, CO: NavPress, 1990.

Malphurs, Aubrey. *A New Kind of Church: Understanding Models of Ministry for 21st Century*. Grand Rapids, MI: Baker Books, 2007.

_____. *The Dynamics of Church Leadership*. Grand Rapids, MI. Baker Books. 2000.

Malphurs, Aubrey. Mancini, Will. *Building Leaders*. Grand Rapids, MI. Baker Books. 2004.

Martin, Glen and Gary McIntosh. *Creating Community: Deeper Fellowship through Small Group Ministry.* Nashville, TN: Broadman & Holman Publishers, 1997.

Maxwell, John C. *Developing the Leader within You.* Nashville, TN: Thomas Nelson, Inc., 1993.

_____. *The 21 Indispensable Qualities of a Leader*. Nashville, TN: Thomas Nelson Publishers, 1999.

Olowe, Abi. *Missional Reformation for Discipling Nations*. Houston, TX: Omega Publishers, 2009.

Powell, Paul W. *Getting the Lead out of Leadership*. Tyler, TX. 1997.

_____. Sanders, J. Oswald. *Spiritual Leadership*. Chicago, IL: Moody Press, 1980.

_____. *Spiritual Discipleship: Principles of following Christ for Every Believer*. Chicago, IL: Moody Publishers, 1990.

Slaughter, Mike. *Change the World: Recovering the Message and Mission of Jesus.* Nashville, TN: Abingdon Press, 2010.

Stanley, Andy and Bill Willits. *Creating Community: 5 Keys to Building a Small Group Culture*. Sisters, OR: Multnomah Publishers, 2004.

Stetzer, Ed and David Putman. *Breaking the Missional Code*. Nashville, TN: B&H Publishing, 2006.

Stetzer, Ed, and Thom S. Rainer. *Transformational Church*. Nashville, TN: B&H Group, 2010.

Towns, Elmer. *Theology for Today*. Belmont, CA. Wadsworth Thomason Learning. 2002.

Towns, Elmer, Ed Stetzer, and Warren Bird. *11 Innovations in the Local Church*. Ventura: CA, Regal Books, 2007.

Towns, Elmer and Ed Stetzer. *Perimeters of Light*. Chicago, IL: Moody Publishers, 2004.

Warren, Rick. *The Purpose Driven Church*. Grand Rapids, MI. Zondervan Publishing. 1995.

Westerhoff, John. *Tomorrow's Church: A Community of Change*. Waco, TX: Word Books Publishers, 2001.

Wilkinson, Bruce. Lecture Handout, "What on Earth is God Doing in My Life?"

AUTHOR

Dr. Victor Oludiran is a teacher of the Word, author, and counselor, who believes in the power of the Word for transformation. He is called to raise disciples of Christ which he does through the ministry's Bible School and other training avenues. Victor holds the D. Min. degree in Pastoral Leadership and Management from Liberty University, Lynchburg Virginia.

Victor is a motivator who helps people to discover and develop their life purpose for fulfillment, believing that if God could transform his own life and use him to preach the gospel that has touched so many lives despite his uninspiring past, there is no one God could not use.

Victor is the senior pastor of Liberty Care International Ministries, Atlanta Georgia, and is married to Bimbo, also a minister of the gospel. They are blessed with four adult children, Wale, Ronke, Yemi, and Doyin, and their spouses.

Other Books by Dr. Victor Oludiran

1. The Power of His Presence
2. The Escape Route
3. Attaining: A Daily Devotional Guide, Vol 1
4. Attaining: A Daily Devotional Guide, Vol 2
5. From the Seed to the Harvest: Discipleship Series
   Book 1: Teaching the New Believer

Made in the USA
San Bernardino, CA
05 October 2015